The Revolutionary
Yardscape

Creatively reused building
materials enliven a small corner
garden with strong color and
bold shapes.

The Revolutionary Yardscape

Ideas for Repurposing Local Materials to Create Containers, Pathways, Lighting, and More

Matthew Levesque

Timber Press
Portland ■ London

Frontispiece and chapter-opening photographs are by Saxon Holt.
All other photographs are by Matthew Levesque unless otherwise credited.

Design by Jane Jeszeck/Jigsaw, www.jigsawseattle.com

Published in 2010 by Timber Press, Inc.

The Haseltine Building
133 S.W. Second Avenue, Suite 450
Portland, Oregon 97204-3527
www.timberpress.com

2 The Quadrant
135 Salusbury Road
London NW6 6RJ
www.timberpress.co.uk

Printed in China

Library of Congress Cataloging-in-Publication Data

Levesque, Matthew.
  The revolutionary yardscape : ideas for repurposing local materials to
  create containers, pathways, lighting, and more / Matthew Levesque.
      p. cm.
  Includes bibliographical references and index.
  ISBN 978-0-88192-997-3
  1. Garden ornaments and furniture--Design and construction.
    2. Garden structures--Designs and construction. I. Title.
  SB473.5.L48 2010
  684.1'8--dc22
                          2010021168

A catalog record for this book is also available from the British Library.

To Nancy B. Levesque and Betty L. Murphy

CONTENTS

PREFACE AND ACKNOWLEDGMENTS

This book is an invitation to an ongoing exploration of the design options offered by reusing locally available building materials in the garden. It grew out of my work in the nonprofit side of used building material salvage and sales, which I have been engaged in since 1994.

In the course of this work I discovered that no one in the industry was speaking to the garden and landscape community. I set out on a journey to change that, developing a series of lectures and workshops to stimulate a new way of thinking about materials in the landscape. The journey not only changed how a growing number of gardeners perceived used materials, it also changed me. I began to garden.

And I began to see the need for an easy-to-follow, step-by-step guide to entice both the professional and the casual gardener to think creatively about reusing local materials. This book is the result. It begins with a brief look at how we approach materials and design through reuse. A chapter on where and how to look for materials is followed by one on tools to transform the materials—and maybe even you in the process. The remaining chapters describe the different types and applications of reused materials by following the transformation of one small city plot into a garden that fully embraces such materials in its design and construction.

An invitation only gets you to the party; what you do once there is up to you. If you take nothing else away from this book but the willingness to try your hand at reusing local materials in your garden, I will have greatly succeeded.

I would like to acknowledge my wonderful staff at Building REsources for their ongoing support and dedication to finding creative reuse solutions. I also acknowledge and thank my wife, Galen Murphy, for her years of support, Connor Murphy-Levesque for his unerring eye on both camera and computer, and Tommy Sanchez for his willingness to build from scratch whatever I had hatched the night before.

1

SLIPPING AND SLIDING TO THE STARTING LINE

The use of reclaimed materials in outdoor spaces is by no means a new practice. Examples run throughout the history of landscaping and gardening. A column borrowed from a temple here, a fountain lifted from some exotic palace over there, and voilà—it's a classic. Today this is the most recognized form of reuse in the garden, because contemporary practice for the most part still follows the old ideas. To confirm this, one has only to look at all the designs featured in the contemporary press that incorporate pavilions, statuary, and furnishings from one exotic locale or another.

Still, most gardeners rely on off-the-shelf solutions when it comes to materials. You can select a period or locale, then go out and buy everything you need to fit that look, all laid out for you in neat little rows.

ABOVE LEFT A selection of plants and toolboxes stand ready to assemble into planters. RIGHT Holes have been drilled in the bottom of the toolbox for drainage.

The advantage is that the materials are uniform, readily available, and easily specified. The disadvantage is that the materials' uniformity, availability, and prebuilt specifics are likely to stop cold any real exploration of material possibilities that might lie beyond the supply store's shelves.

A NEW WORLD OF POSSIBILITIES

Any gardener who has ever been in want of a flowerpot has crossed paths with choice. There are so many pots to choose from, so many shapes and sizes. All those pretty things lined up on the nursery shelves, begging to be taken home and found useful. My advice is let them lie, let the dust settle on them, for there is a whole world of other forms to be found. To unlock that world, the key is reuse of the materials that are local to you.

What is a flowerpot but a hole with a bottom and sides? Through reuse a great many things can fit that description. Take, for example, an empty toolbox. Is it not a hole with a bottom and sides? Will the dirt know the difference? But why use a toolbox? More to the point, why not? Toolboxes are built to be sturdy; they are often colorful and can be had for a pittance at any garage sale.

As the toolbox example illustrates, when I say reuse, I am not referring to the worn-thin conventions of a shabbiness made chic by repetition, where distressed finish and rustification, either original or manufactured, swayed the day. I am talking about the contemporary practice of reuse that embraces exploration of materials and how those materials can and do affect the spaces we build.

WHY REUSE?

Reused materials are generally not standard in size or in practice and therefore can be perceived as hard to use, difficult to specify, and inefficient. So why bother to explore the world of contemporary reuse? You may find yourself motivated by economic, aesthetic, or environmental reasons—or an amalgam of the three.

ABOVE LEFT Toolbox planters, filled with planting mix, await plants. RIGHT We set the tallest plants in the toolboxes first. BELOW Our planters are complete.

Recent decades have seen a growing awareness of the human impact on the environment, leading more and more people to carefully consider the materials we choose for building. The level of economic uncertainty has grown as well, with the indulgences of the waning years of the last century fading away for most of us. For some this has led to a retreat into period or place styles of gardening, or reliance on the off-the-shelf. For others this has led to exploring reuse as a way to rethink how a garden is made—a way to find a new aesthetic rooted in local materials.

If nothing else, reuse is all about having fun. Yes, it conserves energy. Yes, it's an appropriate response to the wastefulness of our disposable times. It can even be seen as an act of sedition, undermining the status quo. But mostly it's about having fun. We get to bring imagination and creativity to the table and indulge in an adult form of play.

ADJUSTING HOW WE THINK ABOUT MATERIALS

While reuse can be great fun, it does require something from us that most other practices do not: it requires us to change how we think about materials and how we interact with them. By this I do not mean we can simply choose a new palette of materials and be done with it. I mean for most of us a real change will take place in how we think about materials, how we design with them, and how this affects the spaces we build.

A garden practice that incorporates reuse as a core approach requires a few adjustments. Time frames get stretched or compressed; adaptation is the rule of the day, every day. You have to develop a real sense of play in order to succeed. Improvisation is no longer left up to musicians but orchestrates material choices and design decisions throughout the landscape.

Reuse is deeply rooted in materials, and it is there we must first look. The trick here is to learn what we are doing when we are doing all that looking.

Our brains know the world by way of analogies. We know what something is or is not by comparing it to some other thing already on file in our memory. This something-is-like-something exchange underlies almost everything we do. We see something and take it into the brain, and the files start to spin until we find the image or idea the brain recognizes as the same or nearly the same. Thinking in terms of analogies is the foundation of thinking about how to reuse materials.

What would happen, though, if when the brain found something similar, it slipped right past it and landed on some other image, one that created a whole new analogy? Visualize a roulette wheel where at the last split second the marble rolls out of the slot where it landed and slips over a couple of

Using slippage in designing is much like a game of three-dimensional free association.

numbers. What would be the result? The result in terms of brain functioning is art, music, advanced science, poetry, and for us, new design criteria.

Science has shown that this is how highly creative people create. They let the mind slip by the obvious answer. They actively cultivate a state where slippage can occur, and then—and this is the important part—they pay attention to what the slippage yields. Using slippage in designing is much like a game of three-dimensional free association. If we use it actively when looking for or at material, it can provide a great many solutions to a single question . . . or lead us to many more questions. Answers are the easy part; it is in learning the right questions that we proceed.

Succulents, phormiums, and other low-water plants mix with reused local materials in the front garden of our example city plot.

Commercial and homemade rain chains come in a variety of forms.

AN EXAMPLE OF SLIPPAGE: THE RAIN CHAIN

One project that illustrates slippage, free association, and improvisation is the construction of a simple rain chain. A rain chain is an alternative to the Western downspout. Both are designed to get water off a roof and onto the ground or into a catch basin. Originally from Japan, where they are called *kusari doi*, rain chains do not attempt to hide the falling water inside a sealed tube. Instead they display it and celebrate it, making a temporary water feature out of every rainfall. Traditionally they consist of small metal cups with holes in the bottom strung one below the other, or of vertically oriented chain links.

Making a rain chain from local reused materials is an excellent way to explore improvisation on a theme. A lot of the materials to construct it can be had very cheaply. Its construction does not require any special tools or knowledge beyond observing how a rain chain works. We know that gravity pulls water down off of roofs, that water likes to stay together, that it gathers and forms larger volumes at the lowest point. We can also observe that water will cling, through surface tension, to surfaces, even vertical surfaces.

Understanding basics like these behind what we are designing is one of the fundamentals of designing for function—which is in turn one of the major components of designing through reuse.

To serve the function of guiding rain off a roof, a typical rain chain is either a series of small basin forms, each spilling down onto the next, or an open cage formed by the chain's links through which the water passes. Through improvisation we can substitute locally available materials that will perform the needed function, even if they do not seem immediately related.

The first solution we come to is usually adaptive, a case of substitution, merely swapping a known form—in this case a commercially available rain chain for a length of hardware store chain. The same result can be had using the lighter-weight chains designed to suspend swag lamps. Because of the smaller link size of this lighting chain, I found it best to double these up.

Having explored the adaptive approaches, I built a second generation of rain chains trading in the standard link form and instead using the idea of the cage as their starting point. The first in a set I designed recast the cage as a series of copper spirals 1½ inches across and roughly 6 inches long, linked end to end. I made these spirals by wrapping heavy copper wire around a broomstick, then bending the ends into loops.

For the third permutation, I slipped right on by the original form to try a new form that would serve the same function. I made a chain of heavy copper wire that eschews the cup or cage in favor of irregular folded forms and angular, asymmetric "links." Despite its wandering away from the original form, it works fine, giving a spectacular water play in heavy rain.

As each one of the chains led me to another, each one spawned a new set of questions. The next set of designs I came up with asked the questions, does it have to be metal at all, and what other materials would work? I tried using the plastic tubing that supplies soda fountains combined with beads and roofing nail washers, and then a more elaborate bead design based on a box kite. This last design came out of finding at a garage sale a carton of small panels composed of beads strung on a grid of wire. Having no immediate need, but interested, I bought them. As I contemplated rain chain designs, these beautiful little panels came back to me. Again relying on the cage idea, I wired them together in an alternating open and closed panel system.

A trash can full of small broken pieces of fired pottery I had to empty out led me to the next variation. Among the shards I found a series of small clay tubes, each glazed and fired. No two were identical, but all were similar in size and scale. They were like oversized beads and quite lovely. I was unable to find what to my mind would be a suitable material to string them on.

Making a rain chain from local reused materials is an excellent way to explore improvisation on a theme.

ABOVE LEFT I rescued these ceramic tubes from a trash can. RIGHT I threaded the tubes onto aluminum wire and looped the wire at the base of each tube. BELOW The ceramic tube rain chain conducts water in an elegant game of now-you-see-me, now-you-don't.

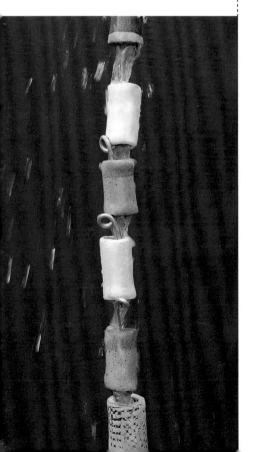

I had visions of heavy, textural cordage all knotted and irregular. I did not find any cords that filled the bill, and besides, I knew deep down that the cord would rob the beads of their inherent tube-ness, so they languished until I slipped past my first idea of them while working with a piece of heavy aluminum wire.

Each tube is now held in place as part of a rain chain by a simple looping of the wire at its base. The loops not only separate the beads but also give more guidance to the flowing water. When this rain chain is hung from the eaves, rainwater flows swiftly down through the tubes and reveals itself at the gaps and loops in an elegant game of now-you-see-me, now-you-don't.

Some time back an acquaintance mentioned to me that his friend had lost his art studio space at a former naval base and had to move everything out very soon. Would I be interested in looking at what he had to get rid of? I asked him what type of work this artist did, and when he told me large-scale architectural copper and glass lighting fixtures, I made an appointment to visit his friend that very afternoon. Upon my arrival, the artist pointed to a pile of boxes by the door and informed me that I should take what I wanted or it was going to be dumped.

I recovered numerous sections of glass cylinders in a variety of sizes. I also found nearly a hundred 4-inch squares with 3-inch holes cut out of them. I asked what they were for and found out that the artist made a lamp requiring a 3-inch-round cap and my treasure was simply the scrap left over from the last production run. I gathered them up, thanked the donor, and took my loot home. After playing around with the copper sheets for a while, I realized that they too could be made into a rain chain. The plates strung end to end made a very decorative chain that now hangs from the gutter of my front roof. They are joined by small handmade brass rings threaded through holes punched in each corner.

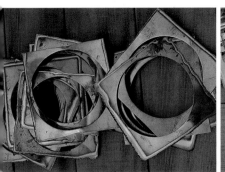 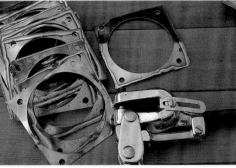 

ABOVE, LEFT TO RIGHT I recovered these scrap copper sections with cutouts from an artist's trash heap. I punched holes in the corners using a lever-action hole punch. I assembled the copper sections using handmade rings. LEFT The finished copper rain chain installed in the garden adds a unique decorative accent.

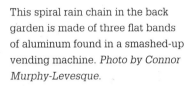

This spiral rain chain in the back garden is made of three flat bands of aluminum found in a smashed-up vending machine. *Photo by Connor Murphy-Levesque.*

FURTHER EXPERIMENTS IN MAKING RAIN CHAINS

Other designs followed, each playing with the concept of the rain chain as cage and developing the idea that the water can be outside of the cage, that if the surface of the chain provides enough texture this alone can be enough to attract and channel the falling water. Form here did not necessarily follow function; instead, following the function to the materials led to a new idea of function. I experimented with directing the moving water in different ways.

One of the most successful experiments uses three large spiral forms hung sequentially. These spirals are composed of a flat band of aluminum ½ inch wide and 1/16 inch thick. You have to learn to look for solutions in strange places. I found these spirals in a smashed-up vending machine dumped along an industrial backstreet. All the candy was gone, as was the coin box, but the perpetrators were kind enough to leave me the spirals. Strung beneath the downspout, they offer a sculptural presence when it's not raining. When rainwater is directed down them, a small-to-moderate flow causes some of the water to drip from rung to rung, while the remainder flows down and around the spirals; a larger flow combines these effects with the addition of the cage form corralling the water.

The last in the rain chain series comes by way of slippage. I was in a rather long line at a grocery store standing behind a fellow with a motorcycle jacket and boots. What intrigued me was the huge set of key chains hanging from his belt. It must have contained several hundred keys, all assigned to different size rings, all linked by more rings and toggles and bottle openers so that the whole thing cascaded down his hip. He made his purchase and it was my turn at the cashier, who very politely asked me if I had found everything I needed. I thought for a moment and then my brain went sliding off somewhere and the first word out of my mouth was *cascade*. You would be surprised how many old keys you can find when you've got your hunting eyes on.

A NEW SET OF HUNTING AND GATHERING SKILLS

The strategies that make the reuse of materials most workable are often the opposite of those required to order "from the book," or directly from a traditional vender. What's needed is a new set of hunting and gathering skills that embrace the idea of holding on to selected materials and waiting for the idea to come through the material. Reuse of local materials encourages designers to look for supplies in nontraditional locations and relies on the concept of collaboration with the material as a design tool.

ABOVE Old keys and heavy copper wire make this rain chain a rough charm. BELOW Rainwater follows the key cascade down.

An active practice in reuse can yield some very handy and quick tools for designing hardscapes. One I have developed over the last few years is what I like to call the theory of any four things. If you have four things that are the same size and shape, you can build lots of different projects: table bases, planters, lamp structures, and support towers for arbors. This list is by no means conclusive but merely an invitation to try your hand at it and find what permutations you arrive at.

The other tool that I find indispensable is the use of thumbnail sketches. These quick, messy little drawings are great at getting your speed up when designing. You will learn to thumbnail with no looking back, letting it all go, turning it inside out or upside down if it helps you. It's important to not make judgments based on the quality of the drawings. Rather, what's important is to just keep drawing. Let your brain wander in the wilds of the materials and don't bring the breadcrumbs with you. You don't necessarily want to find your way back home. I'll say more about these ideas in coming chapters.

THE GARDEN AS ROOM: A TOUR OF WHAT'S TO COME

There are nearly as many design philosophies as there are designers. For the purpose of this book I have chosen to use the idea of the garden as a room. By breaking the garden room down into its constituent elements we can more easily identify those areas where reused materials can be incorporated. This gives us access to confidence, a necessary ingredient in improvisation. This approach also allows us to look separately at different aspects of hardscape and garden design as they are affected by reuse, still knowing that everything fits back into a whole.

I have organized our tour of the garden hardscape starting at the bottom or the floor. After chapters that cover where to find reused materials and how to use tools to reshape them to new purposes, we will explore a number of useful ideas for walking surfaces. Then we will move upward and take on the walls of our garden, whether they are solid, ethereal, or implied. Overhead structures will get their turn as we explore some unusual materials, followed by furnishings. By furnishings I mean all those elements that fill in our space, from planters to seating. And finally we will discuss lighting our garden room. Lighting for a great many is an uncomfortable topic. It's almost as if gardeners are afraid to venture into the very terrain they created after the sun goes down. Who knows what monsters might be lurking in the camellias? We'll attempt to address that phobia with some very easy solutions to living in the dark.

> If you have four things that are the same size and shape, you can build lots of different projects.

BUILD WITH FOUR THINGS:
SOME BEGINNING PROJECTS

Here are some easy projects to help you start seeing the world in terms of the theory of any four things. You will soon learn to think in terms of creative reuse whenever four cast-off manufactured objects of the same size and shape cross your path.

Four windows = a table base

To build a window table using the theory of four, use a standard window sash, which is half of a double-hung window (where there are two halves, and the lower part slides up and down in the frame). Each sash has two faces, inside and outside. Each also has a top, a bottom, and two sides. Gather two matching pairs of these and you're ready to go.

The size of the windows will determine the type and size of the table you can make. Low, wide windows up to 20 inches high yield a coffee or cocktail table base. If you want to build a dining table, look for windows that are a minimum of 26 and a maximum of 30 inches high. Display tables or tables suitable for tall stools can be higher.

Be sure to decide on a material to form your tabletop before you begin construction, as this will dictate the maximum width and length of your table base. Possible materials include plain flat panel doors, raised paneled doors with tempered glass overlaid for a smooth surface, lengths of 1-inch-thick boards, packing crate slats, plywood, sheets of tempered glass such as shower doors, and steel plates. For dining tables you need to allow room for people's legs to fit comfortably beneath the top without their knees contacting the base, so the tabletop should overhang the base by 16 inches or more.

To make your table, select two windows as end pieces and two to form the sides. The outside edge of the sides will fit inside and between the faces of the ends. Line up all of your edges square with the frame of the adjoining face, then fasten them in place with screws driven through the frame of the end windows. This will give you a stable box form suitable to support your tabletop.

If your tabletop is wood or steel, you can secure it to the base by running screws down through the material and into the top edge of the window frame below, taking care not to penetrate the window frame so far as to come in contact with the glass. If you find the appearance of the screws unsightly on a wooden top, you can sink the heads below the surface and backfill the resultant hole with some wood putty. Glass tops are traditionally not firmly fixed to the table below but rely on gravity and a measure of care to stay put, but you can use a clear adhesive if you decide a fixed piece of glass is preferable.

Four small windows = a hurricane lamp

If you are fortunate enough to locate two matching pairs of small windows, in the range of 12 to 16 inches tall and not much more than that wide, you can build a dramatic hurricane lamp. The pattern is the same as for a table base; choose two pieces as sides and two pieces as ends.

This small hurricane lamp was built using a rolling corner approach.

Alternatively, if you have four windows of exactly the same size, you can use a staggered, or rolling, corner approach. Start by standing one window on end. Stand the next window on end perpendicular to this first window, with one outside edge falling flush with the outside face of the first window, leaving the exposed edge of the second window showing. Fasten the two pieces tightly together with screws or finish nails. Stand the third piece perpendicular to the second with its outside edge flush with the face of the second window, leaving the outside edge of number three exposed. Fasten as before. Complete the square box by installing the forth piece in the same manner. Put a candle on a firm, safe surface, such as a tile or other nonflammable material, and place the completed window hurricane over it for a warm and interesting glow.

Four shutters or louvered panels = lanterns, arbor supports, storage sheds

Use four matching shutters or wooden louvered doors or window panels for these next projects.

Wooden window louvers in sizes as small as 4 inches wide make great lanterns. Use either of the construction methods already discussed to join four louvered panels at the edges. Make a flameproof bottom from a small piece of aluminum flashing or a large food can lid, cut to size and nailed or stapled to the bottom of the completed lantern. The beauty of using louvered panels for lanterns is that the louvers allow for adjustment of the amount of light they put out. Open them wide for a brighter look, or close them down for a soft, romantic, woody glow.

Larger louvered panels up to 7 feet tall, again fastened into square forms, make good supports for lightweight arbors. They can also be made into small vertical storage sheds, which can be used either singularly or in series. These louvered towers are perfect for keeping rakes, shovels, and brooms out of sight in places where yard or deck space is at a premium. They can also be used to form a divider

A lantern made of wooden window louvers sheds a soft glow.

Wooden window louvers make a convenient shed for garden tools.

between different sections of your garden. Select two matching pieces for the front and back and two pieces to form the sides.

Assemble three of the pieces with small screws or finish nails to form a tall forward-facing U shape. Screw through the back panel into the edges of the side panels. Cut a piece of plywood to form the floor and another to form the roof, or build the base and roof out of boards cut to length. If you want to hide the material the roof and floor are made of, set them flush with the inside top and bottom of the tower and fasten them in place by driving screws through the top and bottom plate of the louvers into the wood. An alternative is to cut the material to the outside dimensions of your louver box, remembering to add the thickness of the fourth wall, which will form your door, and fastening through the roof and floor into the sides of the tower.

Then add the forth piece to form the door. Decide which way you want the door to swing open and affix two or three surface-mounted hinges with the length of the barrel, or rounded center, exactly parallel to the edge of the door. Then fit the door into the front of your louvered box and attach the hinges to the edge of the corresponding side panel. Check to assure that the door swings freely and closes neatly. You can add a latch, and you can paint or stain your new storage tower or leave it as is to weather.

2

THE GOODS AND WHERE TO GET THEM

The question I am most often asked is where to look for materials, particularly when you are just getting started on reusing local materials. My answer is to look for reuse yards first. They are a good source for used building materials. They generally offer goods at reasonable prices, and often the proceeds go to an affiliated nonprofit endeavor. This is a quick place to find beautiful old windows, doors, racks of sheet metal, and other useful stuff.

You can also look at the manufacturing waste stream and at university, hospital, and restaurant supply surplus sales. I will say more about these sources later, but first you must understand that finding materials for reuse in landscape applications is not that difficult.

ABOVE Multipaned windows are plentiful at salvage facilities. RIGHT Steel sheets await a buyer at a reuse yard.

The thing to do is to forget the idea of "suitable" at the outset. You are then free to explore a wide range of materials that you might otherwise not consider at all.

SEEING THE POTENTIAL IN "UNSUITABLE" MATERIALS

I have spoken to many people who come into Building REsources looking for used flagstones for their gardens. When I gesture at a large rack of scrap marble and granite slabs—such as might also be found in the boneyard out behind almost every shop that manufactures or installs countertops—and suggest those for garden use, the reply is often, "You can't use those; those are for kitchens."

Let us consider this for a minute. A flagstone is a flat piece of stone. A slab of marble is a flat piece of stone. Both can be laid down and walked on, and I do not think either stone really cares if it is a countertop or a garden path. Used flagstone is rare and expensive, while marble and granite scrap is readily available and quite cheap. Add to this the wonderful variety of colors available in marble and granite, and to me the choice of which type of stone to use is quite clear.

Still, people have a hard time giving up their preconceptions and will argue that because marble and granite are polished they must be slippery and thus not suitable. These are usually the same folks who look a bit baffled when I tell them that every flat piece of stone I have ever seen has had two sides, and in this case the back side is not polished.

THE ART OF DOWNSTREAM SHOPPING

The example of using marble and granite scrap introduces us to an important concept in sourcing reused materials—the art of downstream shopping. Every company that makes, handles, or processes materials has a steady stream of waste materials, by-products, and/or packaging materials flowing out its back door. When you are seeking materials, this waste stream is an excellent place to wade in and start looking around.

For almost any given material, ask yourself who is going to have it as waste or a by-product. If you need ceramic tile for paving, mosaics, or outdoor counters, forget about the tile shop and think instead of who is likely to have scrap tile. You can get it at a reuse yard, or better yet, find the folks in your community who install tile for a living and ask how they handle their scrap and surplus. If you need brick, who has old bricks that they need to get rid of? More likely than not, it will be the local folks who build replacement chimneys. Another place to try is the fellow who installs new foundations under older homes; he is removing the old foundations, and they are often made of brick.

One important aspect of downstream shopping that has to be understood is that there is often not a direct, or even an apparent, corollary between what you find and what you thought you were looking for. You cannot let that deter you; rather, you have to learn to use it. Much as in hunting and gathering, you must learn to catch what is available and then divine from it a suitable use.

An example of this was my discovery of several hundred ceiling lamps at a reuse yard. The lamps were from a 1970s-era hotel, most likely hallway lighting, each made of a square brass-colored plate on which were mounted four glass cubes. My small side garden in need of a ground cover or paving material benefited from those hotel lights. Thirty of the lamps, when

ABOVE LEFT Scrap stone slabs in a used building materials yard await creative reuse as path and patio material in gardens. ABOVE Racks of ceramic tile in a reuse yard come from the waste stream of subcontractors who install tile in new and remodeled buildings.

disassembled, yielded 120 glass cubes. These glass cubes turned out to be Italian castings about 4 inches square by 3 inches deep with a round hole where the bulb went in. Bedded on sand, these glass cubes were backfilled with tumbled glass gravel. They became, in part, the inspiration for how the small side garden developed.

Downstream shopping doesn't always mean shopping in the traditional sense; sometimes it's just being open to materials when they become available. A neighbor's new cedar fence becomes your small pile of beautiful but short boards. What to make of them is up in the air, but it will come to you.

Reuse is about patience. Sometimes it takes just that to build what you do not yet have in mind. One piece will lead to the next and the next, until you realize you have a whole selection of materials and every one of them is round and they all want to become a small patio. Or you find a pallet of corner bricks, and the ideas just come rushing at you all at once. Are they stacked into a beehive like candleholders? Are they a ground cover like a village of little roofs with a dusky blue fescue sprouting from under every eave? You ask yourself, until you are almost dizzy from it, are they this or that or some other thing?

TOP These hotel ceiling fixtures were a great find at a reuse yard. ABOVE When disassembled from the ceiling fixtures, these glass cubes seemed to me to have great potential as a paving material. RIGHT Bedded in sand and backfilled with tumbled glass gravel, the cubes make an attractive ground cover in my small side garden.

TAKE CARE OF YOUR SOURCES

A pallet of veneer-style corner bricks waits in a reuse yard for someone to come along and have a creative idea.

Can you see the whimsy lying in wait in this rack of salvaged pipe at a reuse yard?

This PVC conduit has been cut to length for a paving project.

When you are shopping downstream, remember that the people you are buying from or making arrangements with may not share your enthusiasm. They may fail to see the whimsy lying in wait in a rack of pipes. To them it's another day at work, and your crawling around in their dumpster is not making their day any easier. You have to learn to take care of your sources.

Do not be a flake in this area. You do not have to haggle over every nickel, or wheel and deal them to the point of exhaustion. People don't much care for hagglers and won't go out of their way to help them. Be up front about what you can and cannot do. If you say you're going to show up, show up. Show up with the right equipment and the right vehicle for the task at hand. I have yet to meet a business person who wants to assume the liability of your driving off their property with something the size of a small elephant tied to the top of your subcompact with a bungee cord and bits of twine.

If you take care of your sources, great things can come out of it. I once bought some 4-inch diameter pipe to make a drainage walkway out of and was not looking forward to having to cut it into 5-inch lengths. The fellows there offered to do it for me on the spot. All it cost me was the price of a six-pack of decent beer and some goodwill.

RIGHT This selection of round elements is being saved for a paving project in my garden. FAR RIGHT This stack of leftover short cedar boards can surely be used for *something*, even if it's not yet clear what. BELOW This steel skeleton is awaiting installation as part of a fencing or screen project.

A FEW MULTIFUNCTIONAL MATERIALS

If you are really hunting downstream, a lot of materials will go by that you cannot think of a use for. Sometimes the form suggests the function; other times, a form has so many potential functions that you are left with some hard choices. A few of my favorite versatile materials are described here to help you start seeing the design potential in waste and cast-off stuff.

Steel skeletons

One favorite material that offers a wide variety of functions and a wealth of available patterns within a single flat plane is the steel skeleton. *Skeleton* is what the metal-cutting trade calls a piece of leftover steel plate that has had shapes cut out of it. This process is done with either laser cutters or very fine streams of water at very high pressure. The end result is cleanly formed cut-out pieces, like sugar cookies cut out with a cookie cutter. But unlike the baker, who can pat the waste from a used sheet of dough back into a ball, roll it out again, and get a few more cookies out of it, the steel cutter must scrap out the skeletons with their various patterns of solids and shapely voids.

Depending on the thickness of the steel plate, skeletons have a wide range of applications. They make excellent paving sections, where the voids can be backfilled with gravel, tumbled glass, or similar material, or planted with low-growing, walking-resistant ground covers. Skeletons also lend themselves to being made into screens, fences, railings, and

WHAT WILL THE NEIGHBORS THINK?

Hunting for and gathering materials and then saving them for that perfect project involves some measure of what can best be described as hoarding. No one sets out to be a hoarder; it just creeps up on you when you're not paying attention. As a charter member of the Over-Gatherers and Collectors of North America Society, I know this from experience. Hoarding can be seen as a less-than-desirable practice by doctors, your neighbors, your family (spouses in particular), and even certain municipal entities if it gets out of hand.

The trick to gathering materials without becoming socially undesirable is to first understand some basics. The first and foremost is that there is far more material floating around, however desirable it might be, than you could use in several lifetimes. Learn to walk away. Learn to let go. If the material you find is so exciting that ideas are flying off it like shooting stars, write them down in a notebook. Notebooks are small and easy to store; materials are not. If you review your notebook ideas periodically, you may find that some of those sparks have now fizzled.

If you do not have a realistic need for the material or an idea for a readily doable project that can be completed within six months, do not take the material. Only gather material for one or two projects at a time. Any more than this becomes a burden. It first becomes a burden on your own creativity and then goes on to burden others. Do not take this burden on. If your collecting goes unchecked, running out of storage space will be the least of your problems.

Overzealous collecting defeats the entire idea of reuse. The operative term here is *reuse*, not storage. Some folks get so wrapped up in collecting that they have no idea what they have at all. Things get buried under other things and forgotten by the hoarder but not by anyone else. Learn to get rid of stuff that you have not used.

If you have to store materials, store them neatly. If the thought even crosses your mind that you should rent a storage space to hold your materials-in-waiting, alarm bells should be sounding. Unless the cost of the materials far outweighs the cost of the storage unit, or you have no other practical solution to keeping materials clean, safe, and tidy, rental units are a dangerous option. They tend to invite excess, to put it bluntly. Storage spaces are temples to excess, to put it even more bluntly.

If materials are to be stored in boxes or cartons, label the contents and put the date on the exterior where it can be plainly read. Store only the most valuable materials; the rest of them can be found almost anytime you need them. If you need to store materials out on the driveway, do so in the neatest manner possible. Cover all exterior materials with a clean tarp and use them promptly.

Remember, a beautiful garden featuring creative reuse will encourage your neighbors to give it a try, whereas a yard full of piled-up scrap material and "I will get to that one of these days" projects has the opposite effect—that of trying your neighbors' patience and your community's goodwill.

This eye-catching door panel is done in flashing and aluminum banding.

other divisional structures. Small sections can be incorporated into exterior lighting schemes.

To locate skeletons, one needs to shop downstream. Look for shops that specialize in industrial laser cutting or do custom water-jet cutting. These businesses may sometimes also be found as parts manufacturing firms. These folks are business people, so be prepared to act accordingly. Find out what the local price for scrap steel is and be prepared to pay more than that amount, particularly for small loads.

Skeletons are a versatile, solid, beautiful material. The heavy steel imparts a sense of permanence, similar to what one feels when working with stone.

Industrial banding

Permanence may be seen as a desirable trait in a material, but we cannot let it blind us to the uses of material that might at first seem temporal or of little commercial value. Sometimes it's not the present but the wrapping paper and the ribbon that provides the most fun.

A commonly overlooked group of materials for creative reuse is postindustrial packaging material. Of particular interest are the various straps, wires, and bands that hold crates and cartons together. Industrial banding comes in three general categories: steel, aluminum, and plastic. All three have their uses.

Steel and aluminum banding makes an excellent material for woven panels. These panels can be used for fencing, large basket forms, screen sections, and surface treatments for garden gates, doors, and shed walls. Some care should be used in handling these materials in that they are very thin and can be sharp at the cut ends and edges.

Plastic banding not only lends itself to all the same uses but has the added benefits of being far gentler on the hands and increasingly more available. Black, white, and yellow are the most common colors, with a semi-translucent uncolored version a distant fourth. As your hunting and gathering skills increase, you might start finding partial or complete rolls of this material around. I have found plastic banding to have a huge potential that has barely been explored. Later in the book we will look at one novel use for this humble plastic material.

ABOVE This black pallet strapping has been cut to random lengths for a project that will be described in a later chapter.

LEFT AND BELOW This mystery material turned out to be textured plastic landscape fabric.

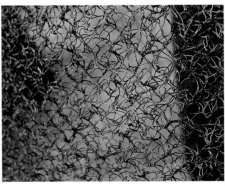

The fabric has a transformative effect when draped over my old wooden fence. I later finished it with a strip of painted trim.

Plastics

Plastics have found their way into a great many aspects of the landscape trade, and some of these products may offer interesting results, particularly when used in unanticipated ways. A garage sale I went to yielded a roll 4 feet in diameter of 3-foot-wide black plastic mesh fabric. The exterior surface consisted of coarse, squiggly fibers like loose steel wool. The seller had no idea what it was, only that her brother, a landscaper, had left it in her garage for years, and she wanted the space back.

Five dollars later I was on the Internet finding out that the mesh fabric was designed to hold grass roots in place on steep slopes. I have no grass lawn, nor hill on which to plant it, but I was intrigued by the mesh's industrial black lace effect. Used as an overlay on an older wooden fence in my yard and topped with painted trim, it proved to be a transformative and versatile material.

Aluminum flashing and tubing

Other materials abound that although designed for one function can lend themselves to quite a number of others. One of those versatile materials is aluminum flashing. Flashing is a roofing industry material used to waterproof areas where water is most likely to travel, predominantly those places where two or more planes meet. It is installed under the roofing, where it forms an impenetrable surface that channels water down and away from sensitive seams. It is also one of those materials that is readily available, fairly cheap, and ever so ready to take on other roles.

Available in widths ranging from 4 to 24 inches, aluminum flashing is easy to cut and install. Used as a wall treatment or woven into decorative panels for fence or gate surfaces, it can be installed with as little as a good stapler. Twisted into organic curves around a simple light, it can become a dramatic focal point. An excellent substitute for other laminates, it can be used on outdoor tables and counters, where it will weather to a soft silvery grey. Flashing can be cut, punched, pinched, and folded into thousands of forms. Any scraps that you might generate are also 100 percent recyclable.

Another form of aluminum that offers a great deal of design potential is thin-wall tubing. This material is most often used in refrigeration and specialty plumbing applications such as water feeds for icemakers and dishwashers. Easily bent and twisted by hand, the tubing is ideal for designs that call for organic curves. Aluminum tubing is available in several sizes but is most commonly found in a diameter of ⅜ inch and in rolls of 25 feet. I have found this product in a couple of reuse yards, though not always in a full-length roll. Tubing is an excellent material where the need for a larger profile and lighter weight prohibit the use of solid stock aluminum wire.

Parts and pieces of larger assemblages

Just about every constituent part of a house, building, or mechanical system can be reused in landscape applications. Chimney flue liners, ball float covers, boiler bodies—all have a range of possible uses limited only by your imagination. Chimney flues have been used to make vertical planters, table bases, bollards, and, cut into short sections and stacked one atop the other, wine racks and breezeway screens. Ball float covers can become planters, light fixtures, or the stepped spillways for a small water feature. Boiler bodies

A coil of aluminum tubing awaits installation on an arbor in my yard.

spend most of their life hidden from view, their patinas and textural effects lost in the dark bellies of large building boilers where their mass helps regulate the heat. Freed from service in the boiler room, they become sculptural presences or retaining wall sections or fountain parts.

I once located two 5-gallon buckets of cheap imported sliding casement window hinges at one reuse yard. Donated some months before, they had proved to be very slow sellers for the shop even though they were brand new. The clerk told me if no one bought them soon, they would be sold as scrap steel. I do not have enough windows in my house to use but the smallest fraction of the hinges and was not sure the quality was worth installing, but unlike other prospective buyers I was shopping for design ideas and the hinges had that written all over them. Slide hinges move at odd angles to themselves and come equipped with predrilled holes. The holes are designed for the hinges to be screwed to a window frame, but who is to say for what other purpose they might be used? For double the price of scrap, the hinges were a great deal for such a promising exploration of form and function. Later in the book you will see how these hinges became part of my yard makeover.

For every part or piece, some patience and perseverance will free it up to become some other thing. Some things will come to the fore immediately, like a pile of large timbers that cry out to become archways and arbors and stairways with integrated benches. Some materials were just

TOP What will this terracotta chimney flue available in a reuse yard become? ABOVE Two handsome machine parts await creative reuse at Building REsources. RIGHT Separated sections of boiler core make interesting accent pieces.

made to be seen as beautiful and will continue to find use, like the set of old iron bars that once covered a bank teller's window—but these are the low-hanging fruit.

The materials that hold the most promise are the ones you see that make you muse, how can I use that? How can I replicate that effect? You look at the light falling through an open-ended box of glass panes, you see how the light is changed by its journey, you see the form it makes, and suddenly the idea is there and you have to chase it, bring it out, and make it shine.

ABOVE, LEFT TO RIGHT Light filtering through a rack of shelving glass might suddenly spark a reuse idea. Buckets of surplus casement window hinges present an interesting design challenge. These large timbers from a salvage yard might end up as garden benches. BELOW Cast iron grilles from a bank teller's window are rare finds.

MORE MATERIAL IDEAS: GABION-BASED DESIGNS

The quest to reuse materials can lead us by twists and turns to some startling designs, and to some that are dead simple. The gabion is one design element that is starting to work its way into designers' vocabularies. *Gabion* is a French word, most commonly translated as "big basket," followed closely by "cage." Both translations refer to a woven, barred, or mesh structure, normally a closed rectangle in form. Gabions are available commercially and are generally used in retaining structures, where they are filled with stones. Those who travel in mountainous regions may have seen them placed along the roadside to keep rocks from sliding down into the road.

These gabions found next to a dumpster await installation in my garden as a bench.

Gabions lend themselves to many applications other than retaining structures. They can be used as table bases, benches, raised bed structures, garden walls, and supports for overhead structures such as arbors. You can make your own gabions out of most readily available wire mesh. The heavier the contents, the heavier is the wire needed to cage them. I have seen heavy-gauge pet cages used in lieu of a commercial gabion. My favorite gabions are a set of roughly welded open steel boxes that were used to ship stone from China to San Francisco. I found them next to a dumpster, and they have served me as a base for a table, for a set of garden lanterns, and currently for a bench.

The beauty of gabions lies not only in their structure but also in their contents. Stones of various sizes and colors are the most common filling, but this is only a starting point. I have seen them filled with wine bottles, large chunks of slag glass, and decoratively stacked cord wood and small branches. The decorative potential of gabions is an open doorway, waiting only for us to step through it. What about filling them with thrift store dishes or ball forms? As a lighting fixture, gabions could hold a number of glass lighting globes, which can be had quite cheaply in most thrift stores and at reuse centers.

To further explore this last idea, I located several large glass half-spheres roughly 12 inches across, most likely originally from a ceiling fixture. These half-spheres were faceted to resemble cut crystal. After playing with them for a few moments I found no satisfactory way to stack them vertically, nor could I think of an easy way to join them to form a full round object that left any room for the wires and electrical connections necessary to turn them back into lamps. So began a search for full spheres that I could place in my gabion design.

Shelves full of glass lighting shades suggest ideas for filling gabions.

What I found instead was a barrel full of stainless steel and black rubber plumbing hubs. These hubs are designed to join two sections of 12-inch water or waste pipe together. They attach to each end of a pipe by means of a steel belt that can be cinched down to form a waterproof seal. With these hubs in hand I went back to the crystal half-spheres and found that they fit

ABOVE, LEFT TO RIGHT These elegant glass shades that arrived at a salvage yard stacked in crates cry out to be creatively reused. Barrels full of oversized plumbing hubs await buyers. They just happened to fit perfectly with the crystal half-spheres I'd been playing with. OPPOSITE A gabion made of hog wire contains the lamps I assembled from the glass half-spheres and the plumbing hubs.

together perfectly. Wired and provided with lamps, they stack vertically in an open-top gabion made of hog wire (a 4-inch mesh wire used most commonly in reinforcing cement for driveway construction but also an excellent material for making gabions, readily available in most communities and able to support a good amount of weight).

The future of gabion-based design is wide open and should grow as more designers take advantage of these wonderful basket forms. The shape of the container and the contents are both open for exploration.

IMPROVISING ON CONTAINERS AND CONTENTS

The idea of container and contained can be further explored by improvising on container materials. Glass and acrylic tubes can be used as containers, as can net and mesh bags. The idea of sandwiching materials between two glass or acrylic sheets is just starting to be developed for its creative and decorative potentials in lighting, fences, screens, and similar structures.

The container may dictate the outer form, but the contents are what make the design come into its own. This is an area ripe for exploration. As one example, glass disks once destined to become lenses are beautiful objects that in the right container could make a dramatic focal point. Almost anything in multiple can be considered for containment. Look to machine parts, thrift store pottery, marbles, small toys, or oak galls. Even something as overdone as driftwood can take on new forms and new meaning as a filler for a well-designed containment system.

LOOK FOR SURPLUS SALES

Hospitals, universities, and restaurant supply houses all have one thing in common—they all generate surplus, outdated equipment and supplies. These can range from old stoves to last year's model of mass spectrometer. Of interest to the creative gardener and the landscape designer is the wealth of stainless steel implements, equipment, and containers. If durable and shiny are on your spec sheet, find the closest outlet and go shopping.

Amazing forms that can be adapted to lots of uses abound in these places. Giant muffin pans can find a new life as paver molds. Stainless steel equipment designed for sterilizing instruments can make fantastic candleholders. Buckets, sieves, and strainers convert to planters with punch. The wealth of forms and sheer volume of materials in some of these outlets is mind altering. You will find amazing glass vessels, bizarre tangles of tubing, and bins full of electronic parts.

Check with your local university to find out how and when they sell their surplus. This can range from Quonset huts open to the public a couple of days a year to warehouses with regular hours. The same applies to your local hospital. Check with them, particularly when you know they are going to be remodeling or building a new wing. Most used restaurant supply stores are open to the public on a cash-and-carry basis. Check your local listings for shops in your area and keep your eyes out for the real finds.

I bought this amazing selection of stainless steel vessels as surplus, with visions of planters and lanterns swimming in my head.

If you don't have room for large containments, start small. Look for interesting vessels that could be used. Good places to shop for interesting containers and a wealth of other materials are used restaurant supply houses, as well as university and hospital surplus outlets.

OPEN EYES, OPEN MIND

In summary, locating materials for reuse is just a matter of keeping your eyes open. It is also a matter of keeping an open mind. Materials can come from anywhere, almost anytime, if you are tuned in to the hunt and keep your imagination working. Forget what is suitable and focus instead on what is doable, on what is dancing and alive, on what is dreamable. If you imagine and improvise and shop downstream, you are on the journey to rethink the garden.

ABOVE, LEFT A hard-to-find large acrylic tube takes center stage in the back garden. What can we fill it with? RIGHT This pile of unground glass lenses might make an eye-catching filler for the acrylic tube. *Photo by Connor Murphy-Levesque.*

3

MORE THAN YOUR HANDS ALONE

Tools let us do what our hands alone cannot. They form the physical bridge between the brain's desire to create and the material's innate resistance to being altered. Without a lever, we cannot move the world. Without a firm understanding and a comfortable relationship with our tools, we cannot build a garden.

Face it—tools scare a lot of us. Power tools in particular make horrid noises, buck and kick like the electrified ghosts of long-dead mules, and whirl sharp, pointy, menacing steel far too fast and far too close to our fingers. But the same menacing tool that can transfix us into inaction, once understood can transform us into capable, successful designers and builders. The key lies in getting to know which tool to use for which job, and how each of them works.

THREE RULES OF THUMB FOR TOOL USE

The first rule of thumb when it comes to choosing a tool, any tool, is to match the tool to the job. This applies not only to tools in the proper sense of something we operate with our hands, but also to those myriad processes that allow us to transform materials from one form to another. These too are tools in a true sense. Do not get in the habit of trying to make a tool do what it was not designed to do. This is a common problem, in part because we usually don't stop to think the process through. Each tool is a culmination, a bundle of answers to a specific set of questions.

Each tool is designed to give the maximum effect for the minimum amount of effort for a specific set of tasks. If you use a tool designed to give a clean cleft and lift of soil, such as your garden spade, as a pry bar to lift heavy slabs of concrete walkway, something will go amiss. It might be the handle of the spade or it might be your back, but something is not going to do well under these conditions. If you need to pry up cement, borrow, rent, or buy a large steel pry bar and find a chunk of wood to use as a fulcrum. Save the spade, save your back, save time, and get the job done right.

The second rule of thumb is to not skimp on tools, as this will slow you down, frustrate you, and make you feel as if you should never have tackled the project in the first place. Get the tools you need, and learn to use each

USE YOUR LEVERAGE

Learn about leverage and how to use it for safety. When it comes to wrestling large, heavy objects such as stone blocks or steel sheets into position, you do not have to be big or even particularly strong. You just need a big stick and a fulcrum, or a ramp and a rope. The bigger the load, the longer the lever you need, and make sure your lever is strong enough to bear the weight.

When it comes to moving heavy objects, don't overload yourself, your tool, or your vehi-cle. To move heavy loads across a reasonably flat surface, do it Egyptian style. Use three or more lengths of ABS, steel, or PVC pipe as rollers, and a sturdy lever. Stick the lever under the rear of the load and lift up on the long end. When you have rolled past the first pipe, move it to the front and put it under the load. Keep repeating this process. This is easy to do with two or more people but can also be effective as a solo act.

A BASIC TOOL KIT

A basic tool kit for working with reused material in the landscape should include the following items:

- **Hammer.** Check out the new titanium super-light models, for less weight and less fatigue.
- **Level.** Get a good one and it will last.
- **Square.** The aluminum triangle versions are great for quick layouts.
- **Drill.** A general-purpose cordless drill is a good starting point.
- **Magnetic bit holder.** This turns your drill into a power screwdriver. The versions with a sliding tube for holding screws in alignment allow for one-handed control, freeing your other hand to hold the work piece. Tips of every type are sold separately and should be changed when they become worn.
- **Saw.** A short handsaw or circular saw will do for most projects; add others as needed.
- **Pliers.** The offset channel-lock style are the ones to get. These are great for pulling nails through the backs of boards, as well as the usual uses.
- **Pry bar.** The newer flat bars with a curved profile are the ticket for most jobs.
- **Metal shears.** Long-bladed versions like scissors allow for easy cutting of sheet metals.
- **Gas torch.** You will need one only if you are doing wax-resist patina work.
- **Shovel and/or spade.** There are numerous styles to choose from.
- **Metal rake.** This tool is invaluable for leveling during a paving project.
- **Hand trowel.** You will use this for all those little holes and fill-ins where a shovel is unwieldy.
- **Measuring tape.** Do not use a cloth tape designed for measuring fabric; they are not accurate. For most jobs, a 25-foot tape is plenty long.
- **Safety glasses.** Make sure they are comfortable, or you are less likely to wear them.
- **Work gloves.**

This list is not meant to be a complete reference to all the tools you could use in manipulating used material. Your selection will reflect the projects that you are most interested in pursuing. And at some point, you will invariably need some tool that is not on this list.

new tool safely and competently on scrap material before you wreck that one good piece that will make your garden either sing or cry.

The third rule of thumb is that you really do not have to have all that many tools to do a competent job of designing and building with reused materials. There are some basic tools, and there are tools that do have more than one function simply because they were originally designed that way. See "A Basic Took Kit" for a set of possible starting points. There are many ways to do the same job. Which one you employ will depend on your level of experience, your access to the equipment, and your time frames.

Every project in this book is written at the simplest level so that the largest number of people can find an approach to it. Reuse is about open access; everybody gets to play. Start small and grow into it but do not be squelched. If you read a project description and find yourself thinking, a miter joint would look better here, I can only assume that you have the skills and tools to produce one, and indeed this is what I intended. Build projects using the tools and skills you possess. I have made no attempt to dummy down the projects. Keep in mind that we all must start somewhere, and in this book the simplest level is where we start. Even seemingly complex processes, such as creating custom patinas on steel, can be done using simple tools and materials that you may well already have around the house.

A CLOSER LOOK AT SOME BASIC TOOLS

Not everyone needs to have a truck full of tools. Buy only those tools you really need. Following are descriptions of a few basic tools that will get you started. Remember:

- Tools are specific, so you need to know which materials you will be tackling. What is it you want to do to the material, or what is it you want the material to do?
- Hand tools are slow and less expensive; power tools are fast but cost more.
- Rentals rock, and a few well-chosen tools go a long way.
- Dress safe, work safe, be safe.

Level

Essential for making sure that vertical objects are straight up and down (plumb) and that horizontal surfaces such decks are even and level, the level in one size or another is one of the must-haves for building with reused materials. A very basic tool, the level consists of a rectangular length of metal, wood, or plastic manufactured to have two parallel sides that are completely flat and straight, and into which are set a series of short tubes

> Reuse is about open access; everybody gets to play.

This level is being used to set the height for a "minideck" in my garden.

filled with liquid. Each tube has two parallel lines marked on it. When the bubble in the tube is exactly between the lines, the surface of the tool and whatever piece you are holding it parallel to is level.

Levels come in a number of grades, materials, and price points. They also come in a bewildering number of lengths, ranging from a 10-inch-long torpedo level designed for close work in the plumbing trades to a 6-plus-foot-long cement mason's level. If you are just starting out, the most useful length is a maximum of 2 to 3 feet. I know a number of women in the field who swear by the small torpedo level, saying that the small size, weight, and ease of use outweigh any possible shortcomings in accuracy. They are not alone; a torpedo is often my go-to level.

Either way, get one that is solidly made. The thin plastic styles are less expensive but tend to warp faster than wood or aluminum models. Regardless of the model or style you choose, take good care of your level. Do not store it leaning up against the potting bench or garage wall. Either hang it vertically or store it on edge on a flat dry surface, and your level will give you years of good service.

This combination square is the right tool to mark a cut line on a laminated beam.

Square

Just as a level helps you set things straight, a square in its simplest form allows you to set material at an angle of exactly 90 degrees relative to an existing edge. If, for instance, you are cutting a fence board to length and want the top to be square with (at right angles to) the edges, this is the tool to make that happen. The fact that squares come in a variety of sizes and seemingly disparate shapes is telling. Squares are designed to perform a range of measuring and marking functions, from marking our example fence board to laying out a pitched roof or an angled stairwell.

The most common square, called a combination square, is a flat steel ruler with a sliding head that can be moved to a desired point on the ruler, where it can give the correct layout for either a 90-degree or a 45-degree angle. This tool is more versatile than a fixed-blade square and is generally less expensive. Squares can vary widely in price, depending on the material they are made of, the level of complexity they are designed for, and the degree of accuracy they offer. For most work with reused materials, a standard combination square is more than adequate.

If you are in need of a larger square, say for marking sheet goods like plywood, there are a number of styles of T squares originally designed for the drywall industry that are accurate and reasonably priced. In general I recommend these over a carpenter's framing square, a steel right angle with one 18- and one 24-inch arm, which can easily be inaccurate, particularly when you are just getting started.

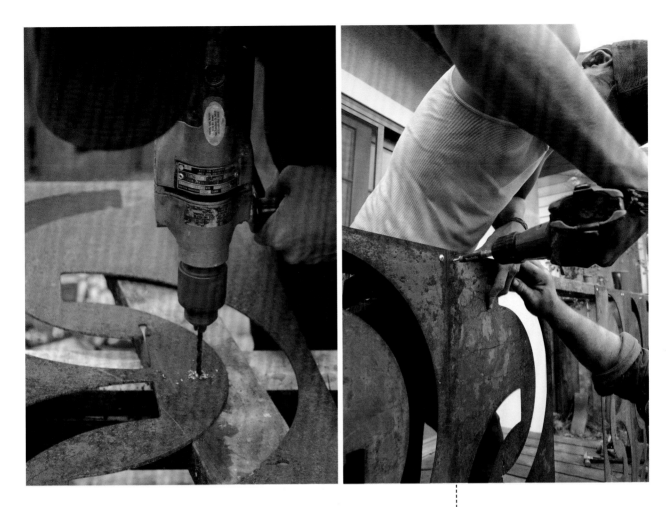

Drill

The next tool to consider for your working arsenal is a good drill. Drills are made for making holes, and that is about it. Despite the fact that numerous attachments can be bought for use with drills, very few are worth the purchase price. The exception to this is the magnetic screwdriver bit holder, which is a marvelous little thing to have in the toolbox.

Drills come in two main categories—plug in, corded styles and cordless units. Within these two groups a number of options are available. Corded drills come in larger sizes with stronger motors and a larger chuck capacity than cordless models. (A drill chuck is the adjustable circular jaw on the front of the drill motor that holds the drill bit or other tool in place.) Drill chucks on corded drills often require a chuck key to loosen or tighten the jaw, while cordless models often forgo this in favor of a hand-gripped "keyless" chuck.

ABOVE, LEFT TO RIGHT **Mounting holes** in steel plate are drilled using a heavy-duty corded drill with a half-inch drive (that is, that holds drill shanks up to ½ inch in diameter). *Photo by Connor Murphy-Levesque.* This cordless drill-driver is just the tool to screw skeletons into position. *Photo by Connor Murphy-Levesque.*

This corded dedicated screw gun made quick work of screwing copper strapping to a hollow beam made from a plastic-and-wood-fiber amalgam but turned out not to be the ideal tool for use with denser materials. *Photo by Connor Murphy-Levesque.*

The deciding factor when choosing a drill is what your needs are. If you are consistently boring holes larger than an inch across, a corded drill is the way to go. If you are doing general light-to-medium-duty drilling and driving screws, a cordless drill might be the better choice. Cordless drills have the advantage of portability and flexibility, in that you are not tethered to one place. The disadvantage of a cordless drill is that the battery will only hold a charge for so long. This can be a drawback on long workdays. Batteries take a couple of hours to charge, so unless you have more than one battery you are forced to have some downtime.

The development of cordless tools has led to a bigger-is-better approach to battery size and consequently to available power. Bigger batteries also weigh more. When buying a drill, be sure to check the weight of the tool with a battery in it. A tool that is too heavy for your comfortable use is of no use at all. I personally use a fairly small lightweight drill, the kind that my carpenter friends laugh at and refer to as a kitchen drawer drill. I remain unfazed and continue to use it, finding the smaller size and lighter weight less tiring.

If your goal is to use the cordless drill mostly for driving in screws, there is another option to consider. The cordless impact driver is a fairly new entry into the field, and I strongly recommend it. A combination of light weight and real driving power make this the tool of choice, particularly for women practitioners. This tool is a real field leveler, making the driving of long fasteners, even in very hard materials, much easier. Even if you are happy with the tool you already own, you should consider giving one of these a try.

The same cannot be said of the dedicated corded screw gun we tried out. It is definitely designed for driving screws into sheetrock or plasterboard and little else. The tool spins a screw so fast that it becomes unmanageable in any but the softest materials. The screw shooter's high speed is coupled with very little torque, making this tool almost useless on dense materials such as older wood or metal. It is definitely of little use in building with reused materials.

Saw

Saws come in so many types and sizes that it would seem there is more than one for every known cutting task. I could spend a very long—and boring—time discussing all of the finer points of the world of saws. In truth, there are only three saws we need concern ourselves with for our purposes—the jigsaw, the circular saw, and the reciprocating saw.

The jigsaw uses a short (2-to-3-inch) blade mounted vertically. Blades are available for wood, metal, and plastics. The real virtue of a jigsaw is that it does not cut straight. In most cases this could be seen as a major drawback, but the jigsaw loves the curvy stuff, the rounded, the filigreed, and the flared. It is very useful, for example, for notching out areas where a pipe will pass through. The small profile of the blade allows for cuts to be made in the center of a work piece without cutting from either edge; to do this, drill a pilot hole, then insert the blade through the hole.

A jigsaw makes fast, easy cuts in steel plates. *Photo by Connor Murphy-Levesque.*

RIGHT A 12-inch blade on a miter saw quickly cuts through a composite beam. *Photo by Connor Murphy-Levesque.* BELOW Making repetitive cuts is easy when using a stop on the saw table.

There are some cordless versions of the jigsaw, but I have not found one that can match the usefulness of a corded version. The same holds true for circular saws.

The circular saw is the workhorse of the power-saw family. Available in several blade sizes, this versatile tool is used for crosscutting lumber as well as ripping down the length of lumber and plywood. A larger blade size is generally accompanied by larger overall dimensions. The standard blade size for circular saws is 7¼ inches. This allows for a maximum depth of cut of just less than 3 inches, making it ideal for cutting standard dimensional lumber such as 2x4s.

If you are purchasing a circular saw, it is very important to get one that you are comfortable using. If you do not need the day-in, day-out reliability of a large worm-drive saw ("worm-drive" refers to a drive mechanism that consists of a gear with teeth cut on an angle to be driven by a short revolving screw), with its attendant weight and heavy torque, don't buy one. I often use a much smaller saw for most work, saving my larger saw for cutting marble, steel, and other dense materials. A 5½- or 6-inch blade, originally designed for cutting trim, is an excellent substitute when a larger tool is not needed. This size blade cuts deep enough to tackle a 2x4 and handles plywood equally well. Consider one of these if the other saws seem too heavy or too large for you to handle with ease.

If you are making multiple crosscuts on dimensional lumber, a chop saw can save you time while increasing the accuracy of your work. A chop saw, also referred to as a miter saw, is basically a circular saw mounted on a spring-loaded or sliding bar over a shallow metal table or stand, with a short vertical fence on the rear edge. Weighing in at 25 pounds and up, this is not the saw you turn to for a couple of board's worth of crosscutting; your circular saw is best suited for that. If you are building a deck or a fence or other project where multiple cuts of the same material are the order of the day, the chop saw will save time and labor.

This saw should be used on a flat, level surface set about waist high. Sawhorses and a plank or two will generally suffice. The cutting action is a down-and-across motion, which can seem a little nerve-racking at first. The beauty of the chop saw is that the blade cannot jump up like a circular saw blade. As long as you have a firm grip or a set of clamps on the work piece you are cutting it goes very smoothly. This is not true if you are cutting short pieces of material. Short stock should always be held down with a clamp and never with your hand.

If you are cutting multiple pieces to the same length, a chop saw allows you to set a stop, which keeps material from going past a premeasured point. At its simplest, a stop is a block of wood held in place by a sturdy clamp. The clamp presses the block against the back fence, forming a point

This reciprocating saw was used to remove a narrow end section on a beam.

HOW TO CUT DIFFICULT MATERIALS

Here are some tricks for cutting difficult materials cleanly and safely.

Acrylic or polycarbonate sheets

Put masking tape over the line where you need to cut and cut through the tape with your saw. This will reduce chipping along the cut edge. Be sure to keep the work piece flat, supported from below, stationary, and chatter free.

Steel

Thin stock under ¼ inch can reasonably be cut with a reciprocating saw, a jigsaw, or a circular saw fitted with a specialty metal-cutting abrasive blade. Heavier material can be cut with a handheld electric grinder fitted with a steel cutting wheel, or with a gas cutting torch.

Stone

Marble slabs up to ¾ inch thick can be cut with a circular saw fitted with either a masonry abrasive blade or a diamond-encrusted blade designed for stonework. If you are making multiple cuts, the diamond blade ends up being the better value, safer to work with, and faster. Granite can also be cut in this manner but presents a good deal more resistance to the cutting process.

A fragile acrylic sheet is best cut through a tape strip.

where the material that is being slid down the saw as it is being cut, stops. The distance from the blade to the stop determines how much material is cut away. Most new saws come with clamps designed to act as a stop or hold fast a block of wood for this purpose. Older saws can have the same advantage but often require that you supply your own clamp to keep the stop in place.

The last saw to mention is the reciprocating saw. A reciprocating saw is an elongated tool with a D-shaped handle at the rear and a long thin blade mounted at the front. Because of the tool's weight and the amount of power it delivers, both hands are required to operate it. One hand holds the D-shaped rear handle where the trigger is located and the other supplies both support and cutting control via a grip mounted just behind the front blade guard. Used for taking things apart quickly, this is a favorite saw in the remodeling and demolition contractors' tool kit. Blades range from around 3 to 12 inches in length and are available for wood, wood with nails embedded, most metals, and plastics.

This can be a very aggressive saw, making short work of most tasks. It is perfect for rough cutting old lumber into usable lengths, with the added safety feature of being able to cut nails without bits of saw blade snapping off like errant bullets. It makes a fast and handy tool for pruning large branches. I have even used one equipped with a long, coarse blade to rid a garden of heavy, entrenched roots after a tree was removed. It will also cut steel and plow through heavy ABS and PVC piping.

There are now several good-quality cordless versions on the market. They have the advantage of not being tethered to an outlet and the drawback of limited battery life and lower power. If you are unsure about whether this tool will fit your needs, rent one and try it out first. This holds true for most power tools.

Conduit bender

If you are not bending electrical conduit, a conduit bender is a pretty useless piece of metal. But if you like curvy metal tubes, this is one fun tool.

Conduit benders come in several sizes, based on how large a diameter they will accommodate. The most common sizes of both conduit and bender are ½ inch and ¾ inch. If you buy a new bender, be aware that the handle is sold separately and for some reason seems to cost a king's ransom. Given this, the majority of benders both new and used are fitted with a 24-to-30-inch piece of pipe threaded on one end, which is cheaper than the factory handle and functions exactly the same way, as a lever.

This tool takes some playing with to get the hang of. A good electrician can bend very precisely measured turns. Precision, however, is not everything it's cracked up to be, and loose, loopy, curvy shapes can become more than the sum of their parts.

Gas torch

You will need a gas torch if you are doing wax-resist patina work. (See "Decorate Hose Bollards with a Patina.") The simplest and by far the most available gas torch is comprised of a brass valve and burner assembly that is threaded directly onto a canister of bottled gas. The gas in question is either propane or, if more heat is required, Mapp gas. For our purposes propane

An electrician's conduit bender is the tool you need in order to bend pipes into curves.

A propane torch kit and lighter can be used for many projects, like melting off wax after a patina has been applied.

works just fine and is cheaper and more widely available. Propane canisters come in two basic sizes—a tall thin cylinder about 3 inches across and a shorter, squatter version most often used for powering camp stoves and lanterns. Either size will work with the torch assembly, but the skinny one is a good deal easier to hold onto with one hand.

You can often find old torch assemblies at garage sales, or failing that buy a new one. They come in several grades, with the fancier versions having an internal pisio igniter. This allows you to start the flame with a click of a built-in trigger. These fancier torches are also twice the price of a decent manual torch. Manual torches should not be lit with matches; this is a sure-fire way to burn the living daylights out of your fingers. Use a welder's-style sparker, sold at most hardware stores. The other option is to get a butane lighter that keeps your fingers away from the flame. My personal favorites are the long-stemmed barbecue lighters.

To light a propane torch, first light the butane lighter as directed by the manufacturer, holding it in one hand. Then with the business end facing away from you, slowly open the torch's valve just the smallest bit with your other hand until you hear the quiet hiss of gas. Bring the lighter to the base of the torch's open end. If you have the right flow of gas, the torch will ignite with a flourish of flame right away. If you have too much gas flowing, it will blow out the flame on your lighter. If this happens, turn off the torch immediately and start over.

Once your torch is lit, it is time to dial it in, meaning adjust the flow of gas by opening or closing the valve until the flame burns white to blue, with very little yellow at all. Some people can dial a torch in just by the sound. As the gas rushes forward into flame it will create a distinctive whooshing noise, like your own personal jet engine.

Use extreme caution when handling a torch, and when you set it down, remember that the flame is very hot and it does not take long for it to burn you or a work surface. Steel after you torch it will hold the heat for a good while, much the way a cast iron skillet does. Do not attempt to handle the steel until it is fully cooled.

THE FINISHES AND PATINAS TOOLBOX

Finishing and applying patinas to a building material is, to my way of thinking, just as much of a tool as any other, in that it too makes a bridge between the mind and the material. On the subject of finishes, there are a number of easy-to-use ones that are not toxic or dangerous and that should be in your toolbox.

Simple household items such as salt, vegetable oil, and steel wool can be used to create patinas on metal.

For instance, table salt applied to steel causes oxidization, which causes rust. I am fond of rust and use its amazing range of available hues often, but I rarely use the R word. When asked, I reply, that is not rust, my dear—that is patina. If you are a fan of copper, the salt trick can yield that wonderful verdigris finish without resorting to harsh chemicals. It will take longer to achieve the finish but you don't have any nasty acid to handle and store.

Oil finishes on metal have different but also useful effects. Mineral oil is the traditional choice, but canola oil is also quite versatile as a finish. It may seem unlikely that canola oil would be a useful product in the landscape, but it works quite well for a number of finishes. Canola is one of the few food oils that does not seem to go rancid in the open air. Straight out of the bottle it imparts a subtle and pleasant finish to bare wood and steel. It can act as a carrier for color as well. Mix it with artists' oil paint and you have a lovely stain in a huge range of colors. A similar effect can be had using artists' acyclic colors. The proportions are simple and very flexible. I commonly use a 1-to-2-inch squirt of color per quart of canola oil. Artists traditionally use boiled linseed oil as a carrier, but linseed often contains a number of chemical additives, such as solvents and drying agents, that do not need to find their way into the garden. While oil finishes need to be renewed periodically, the benefits outweigh the drawbacks.

Acrylic paints are nominally water based and can be diluted with plain tap water, making a useful colored wash. The advantage of acrylic paints over oil paints is in drying time and color saturation. Acrylic paints dry much

A rust-water stain applied on a piece of birch plywood gives a weathered effect.

faster and come in colors that are far more densely saturated. They are also cheaper to purchase and easier to clean up after, being water soluble. The drawback to acrylic color washes is that they wear easily and if not sealed can fade quickly. In response to this I have found an alternative to diluting the pigments with plain water.

Artists have at their disposal clear acrylic gel mediums that accept color, offer a choice of gloss degree, and seal the finish against air and light. The problem is that these mediums, while highly effective, are also highly expensive. Cement masons use a product that is designed to seal cement and expedite its curing phase as it hardens to its final state. Upon examining the label for these products, I discovered that the cement sealer is almost identical to the acrylic gel. The differences between the two products come down to the fact that the cement cure-seal compounds are sold in a liquid form and are far and away less expensive.

A little experimenting led me to discover that the concrete sealants take artists' colors almost as well as water, dry clear and hard, and are lightfast. A little further playing revealed the fact that you can build up skeins of color with this solution much the way a watercolor artist builds an image by layering colors one atop another. The cure-seal solutions are very hard wearing, making them suitable for walking surfaces. So instead of pulling out the concrete walkway to install something more colorful, you can now simply change the color of the cement. I have had successful results with this colorful solution on cement, metal, and wood surfaces.

Canola oil makes a good alternative to more toxic chemical finishes for wood.

A last tool in the stain and color toolbox is a dead simple recipe for a weathered look for wood surfaces. If the calm silvery gray of old barn wood appeals to you, here is the recipe. Take any unpainted steel object or scrap material—old nails or worn-out pipe fittings are ideal for this—and put it in a bucket. The bucket should be large enough to hold the steel and a volume of water equivalent to the amount of stain you estimate that you will need. Cover the scrap steel with plain water and let it stand. The strength of the solution will vary depending on the amount of water to steel content and the length of time left standing. The higher the steel content and the longer the time frame, the darker the resultant stain will be. If the level of the water drops as a result of evaporation, simply replace the lost volume with fresh water.

To determine if the stain is ready, remove a small amount of the liquid. It should be a brackish red-brown in color and may not be too pleasing to the nose; this, however, is only a small inconvenience. Use a piece of unpainted wood as a test strip. The wood should be consistent with the material you are building your project out of to assure color fidelity. Using a small brush, sponge, or rag, wipe the surface of the wood with the rusty water and let it dry. In a very short time you will have silvery gray effects on your wood. Continue to apply stain until the desired degree of darkness is achieved. If you run out of stain, simply add more water to your bucket and start a new batch. If you are in a hurry, add a couple of pounds of table salt to the water. When you are finished with your project, remember that even rusty steel is recyclable and handle yours appropriately.

DECORATE HOSE BOLLARDS WITH A PATINA

MATERIALS

- 4-inch-square steel tubes (any length from about 8 inches to about 6 feet)
- steel wool
- a wax candle and matches
- tap water in a sprayer bottle
- table salt
- vegetable oil (optional)

This bollard placed at the intersection of two paths helps guide the errant garden hose around the corner.

A bollard is a solid vertical element like a pipe stuck into the ground. Its main function is to stop or defer movement in a chosen direction. You will often see bollards in front of government offices or at shopping centers, placed to prevent cars from driving directly next to the building or into protected driveways. While primarily a security feature, bollards can also be pressed into service to keep your hose from dragging across your garden beds, particularly when you have to go around a corner.

The steel tubes used to illustrate this project were leftovers that had been cut off a longer length, and I made no attempt to cut them shorter, mainly because steel tubes are difficult to cut. They are tough enough to require special blades on most saws, or a welder's cutting torch. Keeping it simple in this case dictated using the full available length, but not the original color, which was a dull and uninteresting gray brown.

Paint could be applied to the exterior surface, but to actually change the color of the metal itself could require the use of some very strong chemicals. But it need not be so. You can create a beautiful patina of decorative rust with as little as water and some kitchen salt. If you want to create interesting patterns within the patina, a burning wax candle is

A simple wax resist pattern can be applied to steel to create an interesting speckled or flecked finish.

The finished patina on a steel tube offers interesting hues and patterns.

an easily obtained decorative partner. Salt and water cause the metal to oxidize, or rust. Candle wax dripped on the metal resists the salt's corrosive power. Where there is wax sealing out the salt and oxygen, no rust will occur. The process of using wax as a pattern-making resister is very similar to what happens in the creation of batik fabrics.

1. Clean the tubes off with a little steel wool.

2. Light the candle and move it at a 45-degree angle above the metal surface, allowing a liberal amount of wax to drip from the candle. The angle increases the amount of wax that can become liquid at any given time by increasing the surface area being heated. A steeper angle causes the melting wax to extinguish the flame, and a shallower one decreases the wax's flow.

3. After the wax has cooled and hardened, spray the surface of the steel with tap water and cake on a large amount of dry salt. The action of the moisture and salt set the patina on its way.

4. Mist the salted surface frequently with the spray bottle, keeping it moist but not dripping wet for a week or more. In eight to twelve days the patina will have set on the surface and etched itself into the steel.

5. To finish the piece, choose one method: (a) Scrape the wax off with a one-sided razor blade, leaving the non-patinaed surface below exposed. This can then be left to slowly catch up with the rest of the finish, leaving a subtle shading, or sealed with a coat of oil, which will create a sharper contrast on the surface. (b) Melt the excess wax off and burn the remnants into place on the surface of the steel using a gas torch.

A patina that has been sealed in wax that was flamed into place will last a very long time. The wax as it dissolves and lodges in the texture of the steel will also tend to darken the finish slightly. This can leave beautiful effects ranging from subtle patterns of light and dark to large areas of dark against a brighter ground. Experiment with small pieces of steel. Try differing amounts of salt to water to see what works best for you. The same goes for using wax as a resister—play around with it and try different oils, such as canola or mineral oil, for their finish characteristics.

When you are ready to install your bollard, set it in a hole with about a third of the total length below grade, then backfill the hole with dirt. Use a level to make sure the bollard is plumb and straight.

4

WALK ON THIS

Paving in all its varied forms plays several roles in the landscape. The primary one seems to be to keep our shoes clean and dry. The secondary role of paving in the landscape is to direct us, to lead us around the corner, to draw us forward to some vista that we might not have seen had the path not led us to it. Third, paving acts as a unifier, a visual thread that stitches together our vision of the garden.

Paving with reused materials has been practiced for some time. Many a path and patio is made up of a chimney's worth of bricks, or repurposed stone. Broken concrete slabs have found their way into gardens for years as well. Given this long history of reuse, bricks and broken cement do not need a long treatment here. In fact, we are done with them for the most part. There are many other materials

besides these old standbys that we can reuse in order to build beautiful surfaces.

In the preface I promised that we would follow the transformation of one small city plot into a garden that fully embraces reused materials in its design and construction. You have seen glimpses of some of the ingredients of this transformation in the preceding two chapters, but now we will focus in earnest on this transformation from floor to ceiling. The plot in question is my own yard. Although it is a small, unremarkable affair surrounding a modest house, it made for a great test kitchen to try out the various recipes for change. Through the reuse of local materials, it stopped being a rather weedy bit of grass and became a real garden.

ABOVE Cedar boards and steel plate are the materials I chose to build a pathway of. BELOW The area to be paved is cleared of plants and leveled.

FIRST STEPS: A NEW ACCESS PATHWAY

The first paving project I undertook was all about taking advantage of materials that might not normally be considered for the task at hand. I wanted a pathway that would allow deep access into the front garden from the rear sidewalk. I wanted a shortcut to a central watering point so I could avoid having to drag the hose out to, then down the front sidewalk to water the plants on the extreme edge of the property. The path needed to skirt a lime

A steel section is framed to sit flush with two cedar sections. The section will be turned upside down from here and the frame will be fitted into place between two minidecks.

tree while providing convenient spots to pick fruit from. The third design request came from the mail carrier, who wanted an outlet from the back walkway into the neighbor's yard so he could cut across without stepping on the plantings. All of this needed to thread between existing plantings while leaving room for new plants. The budget was the size of a succulent start. Get ready, get set, go.

Any number of materials might have made an interesting solution to the design problem, but I chose two that are not normally used for this type of application—nor are they often used together. The first was scrap

USING THUMBNAILS FOR DESIGN IDEAS

A useful way to play with design ideas and figure out what you want to build is to make thumbnail sketches. All you need is a pencil or pen and a piece of paper. You don't need a sketchbook or anything fancy. If Lincoln's Gettysburg address and the menu from my last dinner party could be done on the back of an envelope, your garden can be thought out on one, too.

Think of the basic shapes of your garden project. Keep it simple and keep it small—hence the name thumbnail—and work fast. Use basic shapes or squiggles to represent your ideas. Keep moving the various design elements around, turn things upside down,

play with different shapes. This is not the time to be stressing on your self-perceived lack of artistic abilities; nobody is ever going to see these little monsters that you are hatching. I promise you that personnel from the Louvre will not break into your house and steal them.

Relax and let fly. Make lots of little doodley drawings that give you an idea for the next little doodley thing, and soon enough you will have one little thumbnail-sized squiggley idea that your eye keeps coming back to. Most likely that is the one, or pretty near it.

ABOVE The small sections help to negotiate changes in grade. RIGHT This view shows the first sections installed from the front sidewalk. *Photo by Connor Murphy-Levesque.* BELOW This view of the finished walkway from the sidewalk shows the variations in levels.

BUILD MINIDECKS AND DUCKBOARDS

Minidecks are small platforms consisting of a support frame to which slats (boards laid flat) are attached by either nails or screws. Lumber can be 1 to 2 inches thick, in whatever width you choose or have available. If your skill level allows you to do a more advanced version of this project, proceed at will.

1. Determine the outside dimensions of the platform.

2. Cut your frame material to the desired lengths. Turn the material on edge and join it by a butt joint (where two pieces butt into each other's business at right angles, forming an L shape). Fasten the pieces together at the joints. Screws will give a tighter bond than nails in this application.

3. Determine which direction the slats will run, then measure and cut to fit.

4. If your slats exceed 24 inches long, add another support to the inside of the box frame, crossing the frame at the center point at right angles to your slats. This will stiffen the slats and keep them from sagging.

5. Attach the slats to the box frame using nails or screws, keeping a uniform gap of no less than $1/8$ inch and no more than $3/8$ inch between each one. This allows the wood to expand and contract without damaging the platform.

6. Sand, stain, or paint as desired.

7. Install on firm, level ground with a good-quality weed barrier laid underneath.

A variation on the minideck idea that is useful for areas that you want to keep lower to the ground is similar to the wooden drain slats that are referred to as duckboards.

The base slats for a section of duckboard are laid out on grade.

1. Determine the outside dimensions of the duckboard.

2. Cut two or more boards to the desired width. These will take the place of a full frame, providing both support from below and a broad nailing surface for the slats above.

3. Lay the support boards flat on the ground, broad face up.

4. Cut your slats to the desired length.

5. Nail the slats directly onto the boards below. Again, it is important to leave uniform spacing between your slats.

6. Install on top of firm, leveled earth with a weed barrier below.

steel plate. The second was boards of beautiful, clear-grained, normally expensive, long-lasting cedar, 1 inch thick by 4 inches wide, in lengths varying from 1 foot to just less than 3 feet. They were the "useless" cut-offs from a neighbor's project. Given the short lengths available, I decided to make the cedar into stepping-stone-like platforms. These little "minidecks" could then be arranged to take advantage of the terrain while providing added visual interest through the repetition of texture. The steel plate gave the needed additional coverage while providing contrast. That just left the question of how to make it all fit together. The answer to that, and a great many other design problems, was only as big as my thumbnail.

After thumbnail sketches revealed that the most pleasing arrangement varied the direction of the cedar slats and interspersed the steel plates while building each section at different heights, the project took off. The completed project features minidecks, flat duck-boardlike sections, and steel plate used both on grade and supported on box frames. The lumber and the steel were both left untreated. The steel will age to a deep plum brown that will contrast with the silvery gray cedar.

NEXT UP: PATIOS OF SCRAP STONE

Stone is available in most landscape supply yards as loose rock or slabs. There are so many types of beautiful

Grout finishes the stone patio.

stone to choose from and they are all so expensive that it can overwhelm your design idea. Do not fear, reuse is here—and there are more ways to get stone than at the landscape supply yard.

Most reuse yards will have a rack or two of scrap marble and granite available. This stone is nominally ¾ inch thick, polished on one side and not on the other. The other sources for this material are the companies that manufacture and sell stone countertops for kitchen and bath. Sheets of stone once installed in your kitchen are famously durable. Back at the shop, that is not quite the case. One wrong move or a little too much pressure from a saw or grinder will find the flaw in the stone, and then it's no longer someone's countertop; it's a pile of beautiful, colorful, and sturdy scrap. The

PAVE WITH MARBLE AND GRANITE SCRAP

The dining patio made of scrap stone provides space for a table, four chairs, and a grill.

Gather your supply of stone, being careful not to overload your vehicle or your back. Stone is heavy; better to make two trips to your stone source than one trip to the mechanic or your chiropractor.

1. Level the area you want to cover. Be sure to consider drainage; rainwater has to be able to run off the finished work, so leave one side lower than the other. The difference in grade does not have to be large; even a half inch of slope in a few feet will get rid of a lot of water.

2. Decide whether you are going to grout between the stones, backfill the gaps with gravel or other decorative material, or plant low ground cover between them. This is an important step in that it determines how you will lay out the stones and what you will lay them on.

3. For grouted designs, install the stone on leveled soil or compacted sand. On a reasonably level surface, an inch of sand is quite

sufficient to get everything pretty level; sloped installations may well require more. For backfilled designs, use a weed-block fabric on top of the soil. For plant-filled designs, use a good-quality soil to set the stone on. (I ended up using just the leveled soil for my project. I had started the project with a layer of weed-block fabric, but abandoned it after it proved too great a hindrance to keeping the stone pieces level. It came down to adding either sand or soil on top of the fabric, which would have defeated its purpose, or abandoning the fabric and accepting the consequences of plant life popping up between the stones. I chose the latter in the spirit that this is after all a garden where things are encouraged to grow.)

4. Smooth, polished side or flat, matte side up? I prefer the polished side in most cases. It does not become all that slippery when wet, which is a common misconception. If you are laying a surface near a pond, or near hose bibs or downspouts, use smaller pieces of stone. This provides a greater number of joints between the stones, which reduce slipping and sliding.

5. Start at an edge and work across the field. Lay the largest pieces first, then fill in with medium pieces, and last add the smallest pieces. This reduces the number of pieces you have to break or shape.

Children love doing this project. Enlist yours or borrow the neighbor's for an hour. The little ones seem to have an innate ability to find the right shape and size to fit, particularly the small pieces.

To change the shape of pieces without cutting requires the following tools: a hammer, work gloves, and a pair of safety glasses. This is an imprecise art with a great number of minor variables and only one great certainty: the stone will not break where you want it to. Marble tends to fracture along the veins, yielding a number of elongated triangular pieces and very sharp little splintery bits that are ruthless on your knees, so keep your breaking area clean. Granite is better for getting squarish but not square shapes out of, as long as you do not mind them being on the small side. Other stones have their foibles as well. It is all in the practice.

6. Grout, backfill, or plant as desired.

If you are going to grout the stone into place, I recommend using just Portland cement. Cement is the biggest consumer of energy during its manufacture of any building product, so use it sparingly. Use dry Portland cement powder and wear a dust mask or respirator, gloves, shoes, and long sleeves. Cement powder is made by cooking all the water out of limestone, leaving just the lime. The lime wants the water back in the worst way, and it will take water wherever it can find it, including from your skin and mucus membranes—hence the safety gear.

Spread a bit of dry cement powder on top of the stones, and with a clean broom gently sweep it into the gaps between the stones. Repeat until the gaps are full of the cement powder and none remains on the surface of the stones. Use a garden hose with a spray attachment. Set the sprayer to the mist setting. Get yourself a beverage to sip on and mist away. The cement will drink up a lot of moisture. Keep it fairly wet for a day or two. The cement will expand and lock the stones into place.

ABOVE LEFT Twelve-inch squares of salvaged perforated steel make great pavers. RIGHT The steel pavers are installed directly on grade.

amount of material generated as scrap either from breakage or the pieces that must be cut away is surprising. There are dumpsters full of this stuff waiting to find a new life in your garden.

My next paving project utilized scrap marble and granite in a jigsaw-puzzle pattern. Why a jigsaw puzzle? Because with scrap pieces you just have to figure out which shape goes next to another shape, and then repeat this process until you have filled the area you want to fill. This reduces or eliminates the need for cutting and offers some interesting choices in terms of design. Do you use only one type or one color of stone? Do you vary between light and dark colors? Is there a pattern to be had out of this? Decisions, decisions, decisions. Use whatever works best for you.

STEEL YOURSELF: WALKWAYS THAT WORK

For a high-traffic dry garden in an industrial area, steel seemed like a good choice of paving material. The steel product used for this installation was ¼-inch-thick perforated plate that had previously been cut into 1-foot squares. In its former life it had been installed over a concrete floor on short welded feet in the boiler room of a housing project. The perforation was a series of small holes about an inch apart that allowed water to pass through to the floor drains below.

In the garden, we installed the plates directly on leveled soil without a weed-block fabric below it. The perforations still act as conduit for water

to pass through where it now can percolate into the soil instead of heading down the drain. The garden is shaded by small trees most of the day. This keeps the steel from becoming too hot to be comfortably walked on.

Steel plate can be installed as a walking surface directly on grade, or it can be raised up to the desired height by building a box frame to fit underneath it. Steel plate can be quite heavy, so be sure your box frame is well built and sturdy enough to support the load. Cutting steel is much harder than cutting wood. An easy way to avoid cutting is to select pieces that are of a workable size when you shop at the salvage yards. If you are unable to cut the material yourself, be sure to factor the cost of having it done into your budget.

MORE IMPROVISING: A COLLAGE OF CIRCLES

Steel plates also make an appearance in this next paving project, along with stone, a little bit of brass, and some glass elements thrown in for good measure. The unifying characteristic of all these materials is that they are circular in shape. They range in size from a 3-foot-diameter steel disk to a brass doorknob. Stone elements include architects' samples, cemetery cores, and a number of marble ringlike pieces. Cemetery cores are round, generally 3 inches across, of various lengths, and are the bit of headstone removed to make a well to accommodate a metal vase. The mysterious off-white marble rings are of unknown origin. The ¾-inch-thick rings have machined

The finished collage of circles, wet with rain, makes an interesting conversation starter.

out, stepped levels like seats in some miniature coliseum. Who knows? All I know is that they are quite lovely, and they are cemented into my garden.

Installation of so many objects with such a broad range of dimensions proved tricky. Weed-block fabric was unwieldy, given the need to level objects ranging from ¼ inch to 8 inches in depth. I opted to install the whole affair in a mixture of six parts sand to one part Portland cement, with the misguided idea that once set it would keep weeds from pushing up through and still be somewhat permeable. This supposition has not been borne out. I have both weeds and poor drainage. One of these days I am going to pull it out and reset it.

This "failure" is an integral part of improvising. I cannot learn what works if I do not give myself room to play and to occasionally fall flat on my

The hose bib area had been let go and needed rethinking.

face. Neighbors have suggested all sorts of cures for the weeds, all involving chemicals of one nasty sort or another. I did find one really useful solution to the weeds popping up amongst the round objects. One of my lovely sisters-in-law hit the nail on the head. "Hot water, boiling hot water, straight out of the teakettle." It works.

A NEW HOSE BIB SURROUND

It is satisfying and grand when something simple works. My next paving project was both simple and effective. I, perhaps like you, had an area around my hose bib that was constantly wet and often muddy. My hose bibs always seem to leak and drip everywhere, like an eighteen-month-old child with a "sippy" cup. There was always extra water around from turning the sprayer on and off, and adequate drainage was the only real solution. Then there was the question of how best to store the hose. Most hose reels on the market do not appeal to me; I find them unattractive and generally cumbersome. I had tried several schemes to alleviate the problem but none worked quite as well as the solution I finally hit upon.

Solving the drainage problem began by excavating about 4 inches of soil from the area nearest the hose bib. I established a perimeter to this area by assembling a row of standing stones, scrap material recovered from monument makers. (Monument makers prefer to be called monument makers rather than headstone makers. I do not have a problem with this, and they

ABOVE LEFT Short sections of plastic pipe are set below grade to facilitate drainage. RIGHT Once filled with pipe sections, the area was backfilled with tumbled dishes.

do not generally have a problem with making their scrap pieces available. This relationship is a good thing because they often have large rectangular pieces available at a reasonable price. The stones stack nicely and offer some interesting textural effects, particularly the pieces that came from the outside edges of the rough blocks.) With this low stone wall defining the paving area, the paving work could begin.

I laid down landscape fabric first to block weeds. Then I installed and leveled short (4-inch) sections of industrial grade (schedule 40) 4-inch-diameter PVC pipe with the outer wall of one tight against the outer wall of the next. This formed a honeycomb pattern set flush to the adjacent sidewalk. Before the entire area was filled with the short pipe sections, I set among them vertically a 2½-foot section of 10-inch steel perforated pipe. I set it into the soil below the excavated level to assure that the pipe remained anchored in the vertical position under horizontal stress. Once it was in place, I installed the remainder of the PVC sections; where a full round would not fit, I put in partial sections, each cut to fit.

Then I backfilled the whole space bound by the stone wall, pouring the backfill material into the PVC tubes and allowing it to fall between them to form a level, walkable surface that offers excellent permeability. For the backfill I used a decorative material that I developed, made out of broken dishes that have been tumbled to give them the feel and appearance of

The hose is kept tidily wound around the central steel drain tower.

beach glass. The tumbling process removes all the sharp edges, leaving a material that is safe to handle and walk on. The material presents an off-white field sprinkled with bits of vibrant color. You could use pea gravel, colored stone, glass marbles, or any other durable non-water-soluble material in its stead.

The honeycomb effect is still visible and helps define the area, while the backfill material provides solid footing even when the area is wet—which is not often anymore. The water drains down through the porous material and the tubes, leaving the space high and dry. The hose wraps loosely around the exterior of the steel perforated section and the spray wand rests easily inside the tube.

TUMBLED DISHES, AS GOOD AS GRAVEL

There was one other area where I wanted to use the tumbled ceramic material. In the rear garden, the space starting next to the rear porch and continuing to the back of the property had been a low deck. It took up a good three-quarters of the available footprint and was looking a bit shabby. I removed a section roughly 6 feet deep abutting the back porch and retained the rest of the deck stretching toward the rear fence. The decking material, while weathered, was still sound for the most part, so I set it aside for later use.

The space available once the deck portion was removed was roughly 6 by 25 feet. I leveled it and covered it in weed-block fabric. I installed a small garden at the far end between the house and an existing shed, bound by a small patio. The opposite end of this rectangular space was given over to a new arbor. The resultant void of 6 by 18 feet was then covered with about an inch of tumbled ceramic material.

The off-white color helps lighten up and define the arbor seating area, and sets off the dark-colored garden on the opposite end. The change in

The area under the arbor is prepared for loose ceramic paving material.

LEFT A close-up shows the colors and textures of the tumbled ceramic dishes. BELOW Tumbled dishes look as good as gravel in the arbor area. *Photo by Saxon Holt.*

Glass block shades from lamps are installed as paving blocks.

elevation from the ceramic surface up to the deck is only a single riser. This small change in elevation, however, helps to define each area while creating a feeling of more space.

PAVING WITH PUNCH: GLASS BLOCKS AND GRANITE

In the small garden at the far end of this newly created space, a different sort of paving was called for. Bound by the house on one side, a fence on another, and a shed at the rear, this small space needed some punch. The predominant hardscape color used in this garden is black. The garden is fronted by a small patio that forms the landing for the porch stairs and provides access to the shed door. This area is paved in black granite and dark green marble scrap. The fence is finished in black materials. The planters and seating are black. The lighting features black rubber and sparkly glass. To tie this garden together, the paving consists of several 12-to-18-inch-long rectangular pieces of granite. These 6-inch-thick slabs are more of the monument scrap I mentioned earlier. These stones were set as stepping-stones oriented parallel to the fence line.

The remainder of the paving is made of 4-inch glass cubes recovered from a number of hotel lighting fixtures, described earlier in Chapter 2. These glass cubes were installed dry, without mortar, edge to edge over landscape fabric topped with sand as a bedding agent and to assure a level

surface. The center voids, where the lightbulbs had fit in, were backfilled with tumbled tempered glass.

Tempered glass when broken forms hundreds of small cubic pieces. The scale of these pieces depends on the thickness of the original glass sheet.

The glass blocks combine with black granite and tumbled tempered glass in the finished installation.

A view of the new paving areas from the front porch encompasses the cedar-and-steel walkway, the new hose bib surround, and the marble mosaic patio. *Photo by Connor Murphy-Levesque.*

The pieces are tumbled to remove any sharp edges, leaving small smooth cubes of glass with a semi-matte finish. A very durable product, tumbled tempered glass can be used for paving, mulches, and increasingly as decorative base material for gas fireplaces. The glass I used for this installation originally had a coppery brown finish; when tumbled it yielded a complex tone that can appear soft ruddy tan to dusky purple, depending on the light. The contrast of the round areas in color sparkling against the grid of clear glass squares, punctuated by the black stepping-stones, gives this installation an almost dressed-for-an-evening-out feel.

A FIRM, FLAT SPOT TO LAND

Other paving opportunities abound. The number of materials available to us is amazing. Look to industrial materials like conveyer belts and other heavy-duty rubber products. What does the aerospace industry have lying around? What is available in the rural areas that can be tried out? Hunt around your locale for interesting alternatives to the old brick, or do something fantastic and contemporary with the old brick.

Either way, we all get to play, and that is the important thing. If we are all free to experiment, to try things out, we can develop new ideas of what a good paving material can be. If you think of it, all it has to be is a firm, flat spot to land your foot and lead your eye. Outside of that, there are no rules that need to be broken, simply because there are no rules.

5

MAKING GOOD NEIGHBORS

As I prepared to write this chapter on fencing, I was caught for a moment in an odd grip. I suddenly flashed on the fact that I really did not know how to narrowly define what a fence is. What is a fence? What makes a fence a fence and not a wall? What makes a wall a wall? It seems like we could wrestle around with all of this for days and still be bored and no closer to building anything. I know this from personal experience. Fences and walls have common features, and it is those features we must distinguish if we wish to move beyond them into open and fertile areas.

We have two alternatives. The first is to grope about in search of something that comes out like this (which must be read aloud in your deepest, most authoritarian tone): "A wall is a solid, integrated volume in both its vertical and horizontal axis, comprised of a material or materials that are contiguous from a below-grade foundation to its apex. The material that comprises it can be either a single mass or the result of unitary construction." This must be followed closely (after a good rattled throat clearing) by: "A fence is an exterior, linear structure that does not necessarily feature a below-grade foundation but is characterized by footed piers supporting a series of vertical supports. These vertical elements are used to carry horizontal members, which in turn support the fabric of the fence, be it slats, mesh, wire, or other material. A fence then can be defined as a linear structure that surrounds, encloses, or divides a garden or property. Its primary function is to contain, frame, or hide from view a selected area."

Or we can take a simple shortcut and say a wall is a solid block of material enclosing space and a fence is a row of vertical posts to which are fastened horizontal strips that hold up vertical boards or wire or iron slats. But really, we have too much playing to do to let ourselves be bogged down in this type of discussion any longer.

FAREWELL, WHITE PICKET FENCE

It might help to start with a standard idealized fence model. Let's use the classic white picket fence, because its simple lines show its construction methods and it has all the necessary elements. We can use this model and then begin the act of improvisation through substitution, using readily available local materials that can be inserted into our picket fence. Substitute steel strips or panels in place of the wood slats, shower doors or other glass panels instead of steel, plastic sheets instead of either. Use colorful broomsticks in place of iron bars, or cut up sections of snow skis to mimic pickets. There are hundreds of variations available to us.

This is another aspect of the garden where learning to play again, to freely improvise, is richly rewarded. Start with what you have available to you. What is around to build with? What can we get by shopping downstream locally? Once you have a feel for what is available, start sketching out ideas. Go crazy on paper; don't worry about how practical an idea is at first, just follow it. See where the material takes you; let the material help find the solution.

A POND WALL OF FOAM AND STUCCO

An example of this improvising with what is available is the small pond surround with stonelike contours that I had built out of expanded styrene foam. The foam was locally available; a large quantity of this material is left

> Use colorful broomsticks in place of iron bars, or cut up sections of snow skis to mimic pickets.

MATERIAL TO CONSIDER FOR FENCES AND SCREENS

Here are just a few ideas to get you started:

- doors of every sort
- windows, with or without glass
- window screens layered up to form interlocking patterns
- open steel wire shelves filled with round white glass globes
- glass shower doors, cheap and uniform
- fiberglass rods
- shovels planted blade up in rows
- woven sections of aluminum pallet strapping
- old surfboards
- aluminum grids from florescent ceiling lights
- monument scrap stone

This low wall is made from large architectural and monument scrap stone.

A dry-stacked wall of smaller monument scrap stone rings the hose bib area.

floating around behind stores in the form of excess packaging. The pond site, tucked into a tight corner, dictated that it have a strong vertical element to it. The wall was designed as an integral portion of the pond when we built the pond.

The pond wall contains foam from TV cartons, stereo gear, wine shipment

ABOVE AND RIGHT Built of stucco-covered polystyrene, this pond surround appears to be stone.

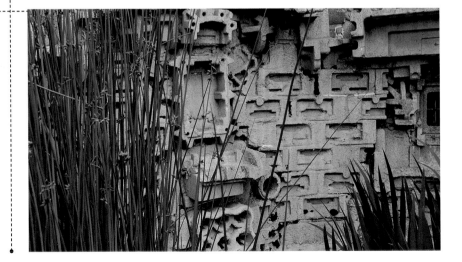

cases, and a myriad of other sources. Two wonderful San Francisco artists, David Erickson and Carrie Nardello, designed and built this piece based on my request for something halfway between my two favorite architects: Frank Lloyd Wright and Dr Seuss. They wired the foam onto a metal grid and then sealed it with a diluted solution of woodworkers' glue. They filled gaps between blocks with expansion foam. The final step was to seal the whole affair with stucco, applied with spray equipment.

JUST THE VERTICALS

Once we have explored the options that substituting materials within the given "ideal fence" format have led us to, the next step is to abandon the constraints of the format itself. We can accomplish this by either eliminating the post, or accentuating the post and eliminating the slats. Look at all the materials that suddenly become available if we build a fence out of just the vertical elements that can be grouped. Vertical timbers and other columnar materials can give form and gravity to a number of settings. Clear Plexiglas or polycarbonate tubes can be used to great effect. The flue baffles from old gas water heaters make for a wonderful combination of wiggly form and deep variegated patina.

An often overlooked but wonderfully pliant material is steel electrical conduit. Scrap and/or used conduit is a regular feature of most commercial building demolitions. It is easily cut with both power and hand saws, and comes in uniform sizes. It can be topped with any number of decorative elements and painted any number of colors. The real beauty of conduit is that it can be bent, twisted, and with a little experience made to do your bidding. The one tool that makes this all possible is a pipe bender, available at most hardware supply houses or any good tool rental facility in your area.

I decided to try building an open-work space divider of bent and twisted conduit at Building REsources. The project used a dozen 10-foot lengths. I did the layout on the ground and developed the pattern by playing with

Reclaimed flue baffles lined up in a row of pots form a temporary construction fence. *Photo by Connor Murphy-Levesque.*

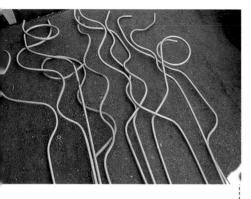

ABOVE The layout for a screen of pipes was done on the ground before installation. RIGHT The finished screen divides the space and breaks up the vista of salvaged goods at Building REsources.

ABOVE AND LEFT Salvaged steel wire ties make a textural screen material when hung in rows.

what shapes the bender would yield. There are a great many more possible shapes to be coaxed out of this tool with practice. The finished screen was installed by driving the straight ends of the conduit into the soil to a depth of 6 to 8 inches. I left the top end of the pipe open, though any number of objects could be attached as a creative finial. I also left the pipes with their original finish, a reflective surface that plays well with light and shade, but color could add some pop and sizzle to this type of installation.

POST-AND-ARCH SCREENS AND FENCING

Returning to our white picket fence model for a moment, another strategy to explore is the use of posts and a single top rail to suspend things from. This arch form can be constructed from any number of materials and used singularly as a dividing screen. How about suspending strings of steel wire ties used by contractors to assemble rebar frames for concrete work? These forms hung side by side in multiples can act as a whole fence structure.

This post-and-arch design makes a versatile form to explore. Sketch out an upside-down U and then consider all the materials that could be suspended from the top rail. Again, start with what is available locally and work your way downstream. Consider materials in panel form that you can suspend so they swing in the breeze. Painted wood, sheet metal, metal skeletons, and window frames can all be employed in this fashion. Look for interesting forms or for elements that when combined make interesting forms.

I built a hanging screen at the rear of a new arbor in my garden using this strategy. Remember those two buckets of metal sliding hinges originally designed for opening casement windows that I picked up cheap in Chapter 2? They seemed to beg to be assembled into a screen that could be suspended. I screwed the screen together through the existing mounting holes. The holes dictated where I could make connections and also informed in part the shapes that resulted. In this way I merely collaborated with the material.

Another option for post-and-arch screens and fencing is the use of fabric panels or sections of billboard vinyl. Consider using strings of objects hung like a beaded curtain. Here is a great way to show off that collection of old painted water valve handles or decorative shovel heads. Try strips of curvy plastic made from scrap acrylic sheet heated and bent. Net shopping bags full of local goodies like seashells or oak galls or machine parts hung in descending rows make a strong visual statement.

This arch form is also very good for incorporating large heavy objects, as the arch itself can be scaled up or down to suit the need. Large machine parts can be quite beautiful, and the arch gives them a great place to hang out.

Large machine parts can be quite beautiful, and the arch gives them a great place to hang out.

ABOVE The patterns of the metal screen were dictated by existing screw holes in the window hinges. LEFT I suspended the screen from the arbor's back rail.

MAKE A DIVIDER OF FABRIC OR STRINGS OF OBJECTS

An easy project using the post-and-arch approach is a simple 6-foot-high-by-4-foot-wide divider made of fabric or stings of objects. Given the exposure to the elements, the fabric in question should be either durable in nature or removable by design. Items that are suitable for stringing will be solid enough to withstand the elements and not so fragile that a good breeze shatters the assembly.

Both the fabric and the strung objects require a good support to make them work. You will need to decide on the material you are going to build with. For this example I use 4x4 wooden posts, although there are many other materials that will work. Steel and plastic pipe are both excellent materials for building arches. Steel or wooden door frames can be reused for lighter-weight hangings. Bent electrical conduit or sections of steel rebar can also be pressed into service for this type of support.

The posts can be set into a hole that is then backfilled with cement, but this requires both a good deal of labor and a fair amount of cement. Instead I would recommend the use of steel saddles. Of all the types on the market, I prefer the ones with four tapering elongated flanges below the square steel post pocket, but any of them will do. These steel saddles allow you to get your project under way quickly and require only a heavy hammer, some exercise for your arms, and a level to install.

To accommodate a 6-foot-long panel, the shortest post you can effectively use will be 6 feet high. The saddle will add an inch or two to this height so that your panel is not dragging on the soil. You might, however, consider making the posts slightly taller, which gives your panel or strung objects a little more room to shine.

For a 4-foot-wide panel, set the saddles with their outside edges 4 feet 7 inches apart. This is because a 4x4 post is in reality a 3½-inch-square post. This position of the saddles allows for the full width of the panel to hang freely between the inner edges of the posts. Once you have set and leveled the saddles, insert the posts into the open saddle tops. Fasten your posts into the saddle using screws. Be sure to level each post both front to back and side to side to assure a straight vertical.

Then you will install the arch, or top piece. You must make a design decision at this juncture—namely, does the arch piece extend past the line of the verticals or does it stop and match flush with the vertical posts? It is simply a matter of looks and will depend on your taste and perhaps a question of continuity with any surrounding features. For my example we will install the arch piece flush to the posts. This means that if the outside edges of our posts are 4 feet 7 inches apart, the arch must be the same length.

Once cut to length, the arch piece must be securely attached. You do not want your lovely fabric or intricate stung object panels to come to ruin by flying off in the first storm of the

season. There are three main ways to secure the arch to the post. The first method involves attaching the arch with long (roughly 6-inch) heavy screws or lag bolts, which have a hexagonal head, from the top down. In the second method, the top piece is attached with shorter screws (about three inches long) toenailed at a 45-degree angle through the upright and then into the top piece from below.

The last method of attachment is with metal straps. This last method is often the easiest to do, makes the strongest joint of the three, and provides another decorative option for your design. Metal straps can be bought at most hardware stores and reuse yards, or you can make your own out of any durable metal that can be drilled to provide holes for the screws to pass through. I saw a wonderful example of this several years ago in rural Washington state, where some enterprising rancher had made all of his fence straps out of what appeared to be decoratively cut-out sections of tin cans. If you've got it, you've got it; if it works, use it.

Once your posts are up and the top of the arch is securely attached, you are ready to hang your panel. If you want to try your hand at strings of objects, do you want to simply tie the string around the top post and let the length fall freely, or do you prefer a tidier look? A tidier look can be achieved by screwing small eyelet hooks neatly spaced into the bottom of the arch section and attaching a single stand to each hook. This is the best approach to take if you intend to take down the strung objects in heavy weather or change out the strings seasonally.

A second method is to drill holes through the top arch just slightly larger than the material you are using to string your objects on. Thread the end of your cord through the holes and secure it at the top with a double knot. If the appearance of the knots bothers you, they can be set below the top level by first sinking slightly larger holes a short distance into the top of the arch and then drilling the remainder of the way through with a drill just slightly larger than your cordage. Once you have tied your double knots they can be pulled down inside the larger section of the hole and remain hidden from view.

Fabric panels involve their own sets of choices. They can be suspend on rods, much like outdoor curtains, which in turn are hung from hooks at either end of the arch piece. This is one of the easiest methods and allows for easy removal of the fabric. If you prefer a looser gathered and draped effect, consider draping a length of fabric just slightly longer than twice the total height of the arch. Place the fabric over the arch so that it hangs down on both sides. Secure it with Velcro strips concealed either on the inside top edges or just below the arch piece. Another similar approach is to use snaps, which need not be hidden but can become part of the whole design. Depending on your taste and the amount of fabric available, you can wrap and drape to your heart's content.

I stapled plastic pallet strapping to 1x2s in rows to form a textural fence skirt.

JUST THE STRINGS

Try out a reductionist strategy: use just the strings and forget the objects. Tie strands of clothesline or other weather-resistant cord around the top rail and let them drape to the ground. Poly strapping material—used to bind heavy boxes and crates, much the way string or wire used to be employed—also works well hung in this fashion. As mentioned in Chapter 2, this material comes in three basic colors; black, white, and yellow. A semi-translucent uncolored version is also available, but I have not yet found any partial rolls next to dumpsters. The black material, I have found in this way and in sufficient quantity that I wanted to exploit it.

I cut the material into random lengths, ranging from about 16 to 30 inches. Grabbing three strands at a time, I folded them roughly in half and stapled each of these swatches to the back of a length of 1x2 lumber. I added the swatches one right next to the other until the whole length of

The skirt touches the soil and wicks water down.

the board was filled. I constructed several lengths of this material, each the length of one leg of a short fence. Then I screwed the lengths to the bottom of the fence, close enough to contact the soil.

As part of the finished fence, the skirtlike poly sections offer a curvy textural effect. This sets the surrounding plants off nicely while adding to the overall ambience of the garden. An added unplanned benefit is that the strapping acts like the fringe on a frontiersman's jacket, directing water down and away from the fence, and in this case right into the planting beds.

FENCE OVERLAYS

Other plastic materials have taken a turn in my garden-fencing schemes, in particular the black plastic fabric found at a garage sale that I described in Chapter 2. Originally designed to give a roothold on steep slopes, it is flat on one side and highly textured on the other. I could not replace the back fence, which was sound but uninteresting, and I did not want to paint it. The black plastic mesh provided the perfect way to update the fence's appearance without any real alteration.

I measured the fabric, cut it, and then stapled it to the top rail so that it hangs in vertical strips from the top rail to grade. I then installed a painted piece of stock over the top edge to hide the staples from view. The black mesh and the painted trim both complement and tie together a selection of small bamboos in pots that border the fence. My wife describes the plastic as industrial lace, not only because of its texture but also owing to the fact that you can still glimpse the original fence beneath it.

ABOVE LEFT I stapled the black landscape fabric to the top rail of the old, uninteresting fence and then draped it for an industrial lace effect. Notice the wainscot of reclaimed copper sheet on the shed wall.
RIGHT I finished the fence section with painted trim and placed bamboos in pots in front of it.

The strategy of overlaying an outmoded wall or fence instead of replacing it embraces the idea of conservation while providing ground for exploration of new decorative effects. I employed this strategy several times in the rear garden. The fence above the line of poly strips is sheathed in black translucent acrylic sheet that I mounted to the original fence structure via screws. The black acrylic allows a shadowy vision of the old grape stakes to be seen beneath it during daylight hours. At night it acts as a perfect foil for the adjacent lighting, bouncing an inviting glow into the rest of the garden.

TOP LEFT Black acrylic sheets were installed over the old fence and stainless steel strips were cut to fit as covers over the exposed wood strips. BOTTOM Alternating bands of aluminum and black acrylic cover the lower shed wall.

I also used scraps of the acrylic combined with aluminum flashing (an old favorite) to add some reflective punch to the shed wall.

Another covering material I am fond of using is copper sheet. While this is a difficult material to obtain and should not be used in soil-contact situations, I find its luster and patinas irresistible. The copper used here at the stair edge and again on the shed wall as a wainscot took some time to collect. In fact, some of these sheets traveled with me from one house to another and one garden to the next. Because copper is so hard to find, I took every

ABOVE Thin sheets of copper were used to seal below the stairs, fastened with screws to the ends of the treads. RIGHT AND BELOW Weathered copper sheets were applied as a wainscot on the shed wall. The warm tone and varied patina of the copper play off new paint and trim colors. Note how the black fence acts as a reflective backdrop to the finished garden.

care during layout and cutting. I installed the copper to take advantage of existing seams, textural areas, and patina. In most cases I deliberately left the sheets rough, with little attempt to hammer them perfectly flat.

STAIR RAIL SCREENS FROM COPPER TUBING

Copper tubing is a far more common material to find at reuse centers than copper sheet. Its use as water feed tubes in numerous mechanical systems such as ice makers and dishwashers means that there are partial coils to be had out there. Copper does have a high scrap value, so you will be in competition with the scrap metal folks as you look for this pliant tubing. I especially love the way copper tubing, and aluminum tubing as well, can be bent into sinuous organic forms. I explored and exploited this property for the screens on the back porch stair railing.

Traditionally cut with a dedicated tubing cutter, copper tube can be worked with a good pair of shears. I don't advocate spending the extra money on a tubing cutter unless you either have a fair amount of work to accomplish or need the tube ends to be cleanly sheared. For my project

Copper tubing of mixed sizes was used to fill in under the stair rails.

I bent the tubing by hand to create an organic vinelike look and interwove each strand of tubing with at least one other for strength. The finished screen is anchored to the post and wood above and below it. *Photo by Connor Murphy-Levesque.*

neither condition applied. The ends when cut with shears tend to flatten out, which I remedied with a quick squeeze of a pair of pliers.

The first few tubes I installed were of a larger diameter than the rest of the stock I had to work with. These became the foundation for the rest in terms of placement and curviness. After setting those, I cut each piece individually, allowing sufficient length to wrap and twist around before finding purchase in a hole on the opposite post. My layout of the tubes took into account that for children's safety no opening should exceed 4 inches.

The installation used five different tube diameters, so each hole had to be drilled on a case-by-case basis so as to be slightly smaller that the diameter of the tube I was working with. I drilled each hole to a depth of 1 inch using a cordless drill and several different drill bits. The slight constriction of the hole allowed most of the tubing to be installed without any adhesives; I simply worked the tube snugly into the hole. If a tube kept coming loose, I squirted a small amount of wood glue into the hole before reinserting the tube.

STEEL SKELETON FENCING

These organically curving railing panels reside on opposite sides of a wonderful reuse material, steel skeletons. As mentioned in Chapter 2, skeletons are the remnant sheets of steel left over after laser or water jet cutters have carved out tool and machine parts, like sheets of cookie dough after a cookie cutter has been used to extract fanciful shapes. Skeletons are prized for their patterns. The steel plate they are cut from can vary, as can the delicacy of the cut-out shapes.

I drilled these skeletons, which I found at a shop that does metal cutting for machine parts, to facilitate mounting to the existing wooden porch

Holes are drilled in the steel skeletons so they can be affixed to the existing porch structure with screws. *Photos by Connor Murphy-Levesque.*

structure with screws. Abutted to each other and affixed at the top and bottom, they form a pleasing pattern. The finish on this screen is no finish at all. The steel is simply being left to weather to a deep plum brown.

GABION WALLS OR FENCES

The next set of ideas takes us in a whole other direction. Here we can explore the boundaries of wall and fence as they mix and meld in the more solid forms of stacked or bound materials. One of the most versatile forms here is the gabion, mentioned earlier in Chapter 2. As you may recall from there, the gabion is literally a large basket or cage that historically was filled with soil or stone and used to reinforce mines and other earthworks. Made of steel mesh or wire grids, the common low rectangular gabion often finds contemporary usage in much the same way. Gabions are strong, stable, and less expensive to build than concrete or stoneworks. They are generally filled

WHAT TO FILL A GABION WITH

- wine bottles
- old canning jars
- short sections of branches stacked in contrasting rows or other patterns
- rubber balls
- squares of packing foam
- seashells
- cobbles
- broken bits of countertop marble and granite
- teacups and other ceramics
- corncobs
- old typewriters
- machine parts
- plastic flowers
- toy cars and trucks
- stones
- cordwood
- paintbrushes
- anything you think might work (you will never know if you do not try)

Who would have thought that a collection of wine bottle corks would someday fill gabions used as screens in the garden? But why not? The corks are waterproof, durable, and sound-absorbing.

with crushed stone of various sizes, then stacked up to the desired height much like stacking bricks. They gain strength from being wired together, thereby forming a near solid mass.

Gabions can be used in nontraditional ways, creating a wonderfully versatile form for the construction of walls, fence lines, and screening structures. They can be constructed in any number of sizes, and no one has yet written a rule book as to what can be put in them. This makes them perfect for building structures such as garden walls, sound breaks, and benches.

You could order premade gabions online, but they are not a difficult thing to construct. Most heavy wire mesh is suitable; the size mesh is dictated only by how big your gabion will be and what it will hold. There a number of common wire meshes around, many named for what they will hold in, such as chicken wire, rabbit wire, and my favorite, hog wire. Interesting to note is that most hog wire is not really used for hogs but for reinforcing concrete in driveways and sidewalks. If your gabion is to be a vertical form, it may need a footing, reinforcing steel bars at the corners, and a heavier grade of wire mesh. If it is a horizontal form, these factors may not come into play at all, and a lighter, more porous mesh can be used.

If you are going to be cutting mesh any heavier than standard chicken wire, the tool for this job is a pair of small-to-medium bolt cutters. Even if you plan to make only a single gabion, the wear and tear on your hands that standard wire cutters or dikes will inflict is measurable. Small bolt cutters give big leverage and make short work out of tough wire products.

Once you have established which type of wire is available to you and how much of it you have to play with, start thinking what you can fill it with. The first question is, of course, what do you have? What is available? Consider that even when filled, gabions allow air to flow through, and depending on your fill material, even light can become a design element.

There are some important things to remember when building with gabions for walls and fences. They must be a stable form. If they are of any substantial height or you are in a windy area, they should be anchored firmly. This can be done by means of a few lengths of rebar pounded into the ground every few feet and then wired to the inside corners of your box or hidden at the midpoint. When stacked, gabions should be slightly wider at the base than at the top. Lighter fill material should be above heavier, denser materials.

Gabions
are perfect
for building
structures such
as garden walls,
sound breaks,
and benches.

6

ARBORS AND OTHER OVER-THE-TOP IDEAS

Some would say the sky is roof enough. They obviously do not live where the sun can beat down on them on a 90-degree-plus day. I am lucky that where I live these hot days are not the rule but rather the exception. Still, a little shade goes a long way.

For years the only shade in my rear garden was provided by what can only, in mixed company, be referred to as a bastard apple tree. It was a gift from my late mother-in-law and promised to bear not just one tasty apple type but an amazing twelve different varieties all at once. My mother-in-law was a woman of her word, but that apple tree was not. I do not get twelve different apples; I get twelve different kinds of virulent suckers and fruit that defies classification. I thought it high time we got a little more shade in the back garden.

ABOVE LEFT Steel saddles are set and leveled to support the arbor's uprights. RIGHT The plastic-and-wood-fiber uprights form a perfect sleeve for wooden 4x4s mounted in the saddles.

I pulled out part of the back deck to make way for a new shade structure and a few other projects. Once the decking and the pier blocks were out of the way, the layout of the arbor could begin.

ON THE LEVEL: GETTING UPRIGHTS IN PLACE

For the uprights I chose a product I normally do not use much of—one of the new plastic-and-wood-fiber amalgams. This stuff does not rot, bears weather tolerably well, and is high in recycled content, all of which are good things. It has the appearance of an artificial, but not too artificial, blonde wood.

I happened on a very reasonably priced supply of it at a reuse yard. They happened upon it because someone dropped it off as a donation. The donor happened upon it, I learned much later, in a rather roundabout way, because it had been recalled by the factory. Seems it was a bad batch. I did not know this heading in and was not alone in this ignorance. Frankly, the stuff worked great and has held up well, and I am quite pleased with it so far. If this is a bad batch, I would very much like to see a good batch.

The material was a hollow tube 4½ inches square, providing a perfect sleeve for a wooden four by four, which made setting the footings a breeze. You need good footings for an arbor in case there is more than a breeze. Without a good footing, your arbor becomes an oversized café table loaded down with plates full of trouble when the wind gets up. Footings can be done a couple of ways for a project like this. I chose the easiest, fastest, and least energy-consumptive way I could find.

Digging a hole, setting your posts, and then mixing up a couple of sacks of concrete mix is overrated. I have found that it is well worth the money to purchase metal saddles for setting posts. The type of saddle employed here requires no concrete and takes just minutes to install. The saddle comes with an 8-inch sleeve that tightens down on and holds a 4x4. The bottom portion of the saddle is a 30-inch four-fluted spike that can be driven into firm soil. This is key, however—it requires firm soil in which to be installed. If you have something that looks like beach sand, do not use these spike-type saddles.

The hollow uprights were installed at right angles to the fence line.

To drive the spikes in, we placed a short piece of 4x4 in each saddle and pounded on this with a sledgehammer. This was to avoid pounding directly on the top of the saddle and mashing it in the process. We quickly discovered that once we pounded the spike in, the 4x4 was not going to come back out. Adjustments were made and soon all five short posts were set onto saddles.

That's right—I elected to use five uprights on this project even though a rectangular form requires only four. One post was installed in each corner for support, and then a fifth post was installed to create a sense of enclosure on the side nearest the back gate. The fifth post sits just at the edge of the walkway, defining an area between the walk and the fence. By installing these two uprights a little less than 2 feet apart I was able to create a good spot for installation of a hanging screen composed of steel wire ties strung in long strands. This screen would then enclose an area where a bench made of steel gabions would be installed under the arbor. Another advantage gained by installing the fifth post was to break up space and selectively frame views into and around the back garden, making a small enclosed area seem a little larger.

We leveled each saddle using one post as a fixed point and then setting a torpedo level on a cord strung taut between posts. This is an important

RIGHT Hand-cut copper straps were used to join the cross members to the uprights. *Photo by Connor Murphy-Levesque.* BELOW The arbor bridges the space from the fence line past the stair landing.

step. If your saddles are not level, you will have to level everything at the top of the post. It is far and away an easier task to set levels while squatting on the ground than to level things atop an 8-foot ladder. Of course, you could also figure out exactly what length each upright has to be cut to so that they all come out at the same height. I have tried this, only once, and believe me—once was one time too many.

We trimmed the uprights to a height of 7 feet—just tall enough to feel cozy beneath and just short enough to squeeze under the lower branches of my beloved apple tree. We sleeved the uprights over the short 4x4s in the saddles, leveled them until plumb (straight up and down on all four sides), and secured them with screws. We then cut the first cross members to fit and installed them using a strap of copper sheet as a connecter plate. This was done to avoid having to leave exposed toe-nailed screws (screws driven in at a 45-degree angle) along the top and bottom edges of each member. We used steel pan-head screws to act as an accent against the dark brown copper.

A ROOF OF ALUMINUM VINES

Once the posts and both front and back horizontals were in place, it came time to decide what to use for the "roof." Ever mindful that reuse is about having fun, I wanted a fun roof for the arbor. Most arbors I have seen use a series of parallel slats as the top members, or a grid of some sort. These are often designed to support vines. I had gathered both copper and aluminum tubing to build the porch stair screens from and in the end used only the copper. This left me with a quantity of ⅜-inch shiny aluminum tubing. The idea of vines kept coming to mind, seducing me with their sinuous curves and go-where-they-may randomness. Aluminum tubing is not unlike a vine.

Starting in one corner and working outward, I bent the aluminum tubing by hand into curved and writhing forms. The aluminum tubing comes in sections 25 feet long, rolled up in coils. To assure that I had enough length to reach from one point to the next, I kept the tubing in a coil, spooling it out as I went. When I reached the other side of the arbor I cut the tube to length, leaving an additional stub of 4 inches to allow for secure

A coil of aluminum tubing begins to form the roof of the arbor.

ABOVE The arbor roof of aluminum tubing mimics the look of sinuous, interwoven vines. OPPOSITE The new arbor shades a comfortable seating area.

anchoring. I anchored the ends by drilling a matching ⅜-inch hole into the tops of the arbor's hollow crossbeams. I found that inserting 4 inches of tubing was quite sufficient to hold the length in place even under the weight of an inquisitive cat or two.

It was a very fun project and a challenging one. The biggest challenge was dealing with my brain, which kept trying to make order out of things. It would show up when I was drilling the mounting holes. I needed these to be at random points along the top rail in order to install the tubing in random organic patterns, yet I had to stop myself quite often from putting in holes at regular intervals. I could intellectualize the need for randomness, but my hands were still running the old patterns. This, I think, is the roof or ceiling we must rise above. If we are to succeed in rethinking the garden, we must rethink ourselves. Old patterns have to yield to more open forms.

MATERIAL FOR BUILDING ARBORS

Columns originated as bundles of branches, hence the stylized acanthus leaves decorating the upper reaches of Greek and Roman columns. Taking a cue from this type of creative reuse of locally available materials, let us imagine the variety of materials we might employ in building arbor supports and toppers.

Uprights

- reclaimed lumber
- tall wire gabions
- bundles of pipes
- short scraps of lumber collaged Louise Nevelson style into columnlike forms
- welded stacks of push lawn mower blade reels
- stacked and laminated granite or marble slabs
- ladders
- scaffolding sections
- culvert pipe
- large diameter drain pipe
- chimney flues threaded over steel pipe and backfilled with cement
- stacks of carpet squares
- steel studs in groups
- machines or machine parts threaded over sturdy pipe supports (I would love to do this with old manual typewriters)

Toppers

- hog wire
- ladders
- thrift store umbrellas
- broom and mop handles
- empty window frames
- window screens stacked and layered
- acrylic scrap, heated, bent, and twisted, then joined together with small bolts
- securely mounted shower doors (these are tempered for strength and safety)
- plywood cut into curvy ribbons mounted on edge
- any sound reclaimed lumber

CHECK BEFORE YOU BUILD

Check your local building code before constructing an arbor. A number of communities have ordinances that stipulate that if the arbor is in direct contact with your house or an outbuilding, it constitutes a change in your square footage. This can affect the materials and methods you are allowed to use. Enlarging your square footage can trigger an expensive design review in some communities and can also increase your property taxes. In most cases, a freestanding arbor is not subject to these regulations. So do check before you build. But once you are cleared for takeoff, do just that—take off and explore what is possible.

7

CONTAIN YOURSELF

Every person who has ever bought a small plant has wrestled with the choice of pots and containers. From little redwood window boxes to the virtual sea of terracotta that floods the shops, we all must choose. I am a firm believer in choice. However, I want more choices, or shall I say other choices, than I am met with at the nurseries. I choose to make my own. Not out of cheapness or stubbornness, but because there is a wealth of very satisfying containers out there waiting to be discovered, repurposed, or fabricated. If you tackle only one project in this book, do make your own container.

Planters, containers, boxes, pots—there are so many names for a nice little spot for some beautiful thing to grow in. To keep it all simple and easy, I am going to refer to the lot of them as containers. I will confess

A polished aluminum pot bought at a hotel surplus sale makes a handsome home for bamboo. *Photo by Connor Murphy-Levesque.*

that I have used a few purpose-made containers here and there around the garden: a sleek pair of spun aluminum pots bought at a hotel surplus sale, a large oval glazed ceramic pot in the front garden filled with *Phyllostachys aurea* (golden bamboo). When I got the ceramic pot it had a very large crack across the bottom and was being disposed of. I simply set the pot in a low hole so that the crack is below grade. Otherwise, almost all my plants live in handmade splendor.

REPURPOSE SOMETHING—ANYTHING

The easiest approach to creating your own containers is to repurpose something. I have had great success with using carpenters' and mechanics' toolboxes as shown in Chapter 1. Old galvanized or rusted buckets make fine containers, as do thrift store cooking woks. Terracotta chimney flues make an especially fine home for succulents.

One of my favorite repurposed containers is a 2-foot-square stainless steel institutional plate cart. It is basically a box on wheels, with a spring-loaded rack inside designed to hold dessert plates, stacked face up, for banquet halls and buffet lines. The more plates you stack into the cart, the further the springs are compressed. As the weight is lessened by removing the top plates, the springs push up the tray so the plates are always right at hand. I played with putting larger plants in the cart as is. The only real

These terracotta chimney flues look like they were made to plant succulents in.

drawback to this plan became apparent when I watered. The water, and a measure of the soil with it, would squeeze past the spring-loaded rack and fill up the bottom, leaving the plants poorer for the loss of both. It also made a heavy, dirty mess to clean up. Given this situation I took the spring-loaded interior rack out of the box, added drain holes with a handy drill, and removed the wheels. The plant stand now has a clean simple look and is quite durable.

I have seen any number of other vessels used. Some are beautiful and thought provoking, some are witty and wonderful, and some are just plain tired. The trick is to pick something that fits your garden, is durable, and, most important, elevates not only your garden but the environment around it. There are wonderful things to use out there that move the discussion about what can be done forward. We should try to make our neighbors glad to live next to a garden that is well thought out, creative, and beautiful.

Look for containers with clean lines, or interesting shapes that can add texture to your garden. They need not already have drainage holes, as these are easy to put in with a drill. They need not even have bottoms, as these can easily be added after the fact. Or the container can be set down into the soil a few inches, negating the need for a bottom at all.

These 6x6 timbers are stacked and ready to build a planting box from.

TIMBER BOXES TO PLANT IN

Sometimes repurposed containers will not provide a large enough planting space. You want something bigger, more garden and less vessel. After all that effort you do not want the garden to end up looking like a used potted plant parking lot. Containers need some blank space around them to show them off to their fullest. Sometimes you need to spread out and cover a large area, and for this application planter boxes and timber boxes better fill the need. For our purposes here a timber box is a raised bed or box form composed of larger, heavier wooden beams.

Wooden timbers have been used to build retaining walls and raised beds, and to form or define the edge of planting areas, for a great many years. Nothing new in this. Timbers are versatile, reasonably priced, and fairly easy to work with. But they offer a great deal more fun when they are nearly free and short. To build a set of planting boxes in my front yard I employed 6x6 fir timbers. The timbers were all less than 6 feet in length, with the majority being less than 4 feet. I had collected them, free, from several sources. Most of them were the cut-off remnants of much longer beams and had been deemed too short for construction uses. Once I had collected enough to start playing with, around seventeen pieces, the project took shape.

The original idea was to form a defined outside edge of the garden where it abutted the neighbor's lawn on one side and the city sidewalk on another. Secondary to that idea was an attempt to bring a sense of

The timber and I settled on this planting box design in the front garden.

enclosure to that side of the property, which faces a fairly busy street. For two or three weeks I arranged the beams in different patterns to see if any of them would meet the stated needs and/or offer some design direction that I had not yet come to. I stacked them, stood them on end, and played pick-up sticks with them, much to the curiosity of neighbors and passerby. I did not cut the beams during this period; I simply let the various lengths suggest patterns that would fit inside the space allotted. In the end the timber and I settled on a series of boxed forms subdivided at right angles. The planting solution this suggested was of monoplanted sections, interspersed with sections of tumbled glass or rock material. Very modern, very right angled, very showcase or shadowbox like.

After removing the sod and other surface plants, I raked the soil level and laid down landscape fabric to keep any unplanned new growth to a minimum. Construction began by establishing the outside corner, next to the sidewalk. This gave me a clean line to run back toward the house along the property line. The timber that would run along the sidewalk went in next, forming in effect a giant backward **L**. Within that form I further divided the construction into three sections that corresponded to the lengths of timber I had left. I divided each of the three sections into smaller sections of either three or five units each. These divisions would be the planting areas and were the product of combining the existing timber lengths at right angles with an eye toward overall balance and pleasing form.

This reduced the number of cuts that would have to be made to five. The 6x6 timbers exceed the depth of cut of a standard circular saw, so I employed a series of rolling cuts.

All joints in this project were done using butt joints and minimum hardware. In this instance I found that 3½-inch screws were sufficient to toenail the beams at the corners. If this project had been on a sloped grade or in

MAKING ROLLING CUTS IN TIMBER

Rolling cuts are necessary whenever you need to shorten a timber that exceeds the depth of cut of a standard circular saw. Here's what to do:

1. Mark all four faces of the beam using a square. Take care that all of the lines meet at the corners.
2. Cut the first face at the maximum depth of the saw blade.
3. Roll the work piece one quarter turn and cut again.
4. Repeat until all four faces of the beam have been cut from edge to edge. The forth cut with a 7¼-inch saw will sever a 6x6 beam.

For beams that exceed 6x6, proceed as above, cutting to maximum depth and then rolling the timber a quarter turn each time. This will leave an uncut square or rectangular section inside the beam. Complete the cut by using a handsaw or reciprocating saw inserted into the existing kerf, or gap left by your power saw blade. Whenever possible, keep your blade flat against the side of the cut nearest the portion you want to use. A rolling cut done in this way will give you a clean, square end with only a hint of a center stub.

a public setting where it would have to endure less-than-gentle traffic, I would have drilled vertically through the beams and pinned them into place with steel rebar or all-thread rods.

When I had built the boxes and done a final bit of leveling of the whole set, the matter of finish came into play. There are roughly three ways to finish wood products in landscape applications: (1) use no finish at all, letting the wood and weather have a go at each other for the duration until one of them gives up; (2) choose from the wide and wild range of commercially available stains, preservatives, varnishes, polyurethanes, oil solutions, and whatnot, which may or may not be safe, prudent, or attractive; or (3) make your own solution. I chose the third option, for three reasons: it was inexpensive, I would know exactly what I was getting, and I could exert a great deal of control over the visual outcome.

I was using a lot of terracotta colors in the rest of the front garden and wanted to continue this with the new timber boxes. For colorant I used standard artists' acrylic paint, in this case raw sienna. A good artist's quality acrylic paint is light fast, fade resistant, and not terribly expensive, and it also dissolves in water. No fumes, no VOCs, no real problems at all. A small amount of paint—I used about three ounces—when diluted in a couple of quarts of water goes a long way. I gave the wood two good coats of color, letting it soak in and dry before repainting.

The beauty of using this paint is that there are hundreds of available colors, yielding thousands of shades. It can even be applied like watercolors in washes if you so choose. Being water based, it does raise the grain slightly, so if you need to you can lightly sand between coats. Once you have achieved the desired color, you can either let it weather or add a layer of protection over the paint. I chose to add a layer of protection to the wood in the form of a water-repellant oil. My oil of choice is canola. Straight off the grocery store shelf, canola oil soaks in well and does not appear to go rancid, or at least gives off no noticeable odor. It won't last forever but is easy to apply—I use a paintbrush—so it can be touched up each year. Oh, and did I mention that it is completely nontoxic?

The modernist grid of the boxes was originally designed to be planted in groupings of the same species with intervals of textural material for contrast. I began plant selection based on this idea, buying specimens in serial. I kept my selection simple, choosing *Phormium tenax* 'Atropurpureum' (purple-red flax) and *Festuca glauca* 'Elijah Blue' (blue fescue). I first started laying out the plants, still in their pots, to get an idea of how the whole thing would work. I tried several dozen arrangements and came to the conclusion

The beauty of using acrylic paint is that there are hundreds of available colors, yielding thousands of shades.

that no matter what order I placed the plants in, the contrast between this planting scheme and the remainder of the garden's scheme was far too great. Faced with this, I did the only logical thing I could do—I scrapped the original idea of mono-planting and got on with the garden.

The beds are now planted with a growing collection of predominantly low-water, low-maintenance specimens, including *Crassula coccinea* 'Campfire' (red crassula), *Leucadendron salignum* (conebush) 'Yaeli', *Senecio vitalis* (blue chalk fingers), and *Miscanthus sinensis* (eulalia or maiden grass) 'Gracillimus'. Several specimens of *Echeveria harmsii* (plush plant) are also finding a home in the beds. A dozen or so smallish one-man rocks, rescued from an abandoned border, now add accents and form a convenient cover over a sewer meter box that fell within the confines of the timber boxes.

TWO FOR ONE: BOLLARD PLANTERS

Opposite the timber boxes I installed one of two small square steel hose bollards. Bollards are normally used to protect buildings from wayward cars, but these little versions have a different agenda, actually two different agendas.

The first is to stand firm against the ravaging effects of the dragged hose. I have snapped the neck of many a poor plant living in the extreme front corner of my garden by dragging the garden hose briskly around the

Another bollard planter keeps the garden hose out of the front garden.

corner from my front walk onto the city sidewalk. Hoses do not naturally bend at 90-degree angles, and it seems will not do so unless forced to. The steel bollard is set almost 10 inches into the soil and packed in there hard. It does not yield to the hose's murderous arcs; instead it makes the hose take a nice orderly right turn, leaving the plantings safe for another day.

The bollards' second agenda is to provide a 4-inch square of available soil at its top. I simply filled the bollard with a good potting mix after I installed it. I then had a small container garden sitting 18 inches or more above the fray.

There are other container materials that afford the same two-for-one results, and sometimes more. Sections of large diameter pipe are great container gardens. The planters I made were constructed out of 12-inch-diameter black PVC pipe. I chose this material for several reasons, of which its color was the first. I have wanted to do a hardscape in black for some time and this seemed the moment. The second reason I chose a plastic pipe over a steel one is that I had never worked with this material at this scale before and it intrigued me. The third and final reason was one part safety and one part sanity. Like the bollards, these planters were going to do at least double duty. The garden they are installed in is a small patch squeezed between the house and the shed, and the garden needed protecting from the shed.

The shed is where I attempt to hide from my wife all the materials I drag home. It is where the ladders live when not in use. The bicycles share space in there with a claw-foot bathtub that I swear I will install soon, as well as an untidy gaggle of construction and yard tools. In short, large and unwieldy objects are quite often coming and going through the shed door, mere inches from the planned garden, and I needed to keep them from straying off the path. If the bollards could keep the hoses out of the front beds, these heavy plastic containers could keep me out of the garden. The plan was that if I got too close they would politely bite my shin, hard enough to stop me

Two bollards planted with *Uniola paniculata* and *Zantedeschia sprengeri* serve to steer large and unwieldy people and objects away from the garden and into the shed. *Photo by Connor Murphy-Levesque.*

but not with the hard, nasty, and quite certainly painful bite a heavy steel pipe version would inflict. The plan worked, except for the last part about their not hurting my shins.

The two bollardlike containers were set below grade and then back-filled with a good grade soil. Specimens of *Uniola paniculata* (sea oat) were settled into the pots along with some *Zantedeschia sprengeri* (hybrid purple calla lily) that tanked within weeks. No matter—the sea oat looks just fine, especially at night when it is backlit.

A pair of custom-built copper and cedar planter boxes surround the plate cart planter in the corner. *Photo by Connor Murphy-Levesque.*

MORE CONTAINER IDEAS

On the far side of the back garden, standing like quotation marks around the stainless steel plate cart, are two matching containers. These were made of exterior-grade marine plywood, which is designed to resist moisture. The boxes are covered in rough sheets of patined copper and trimmed out in what had been grape stakes from a fence. At once both rustic and up to date, they were made for a display garden at a flower and garden show where they were filled with tall grasses of a half dozen varieties. They are now playing host to some young, recently rescued bamboos that are still quite sullen and will not tell us their names. I am told by competent authorities down at the local Bamboo Society that these callow youths will grow out of this phase and will soon be taking over the living room.

Several of the metal containers in the back garden were made out of expired oxygen tanks. These large tanks are used along with acetylene tanks by welders to feed their cutting torches. The tanks can be used for only so many years and then must be retired. If you want to make containers out of tanks, you must keep several important factors in mind. First, never use acetylene tanks. A highly flammable and unstable gas, acetylene requires a tank that is filled completely with a dense, solid absorbent material. Even if you could safely cut one of these tanks, the gas will still have permeated every square inch of the absorbent, leaving dangerous and nasty-smelling fumes. Even if you could devise some way to remove the absorbent, you would still have toxic material to dispose of. Leave well enough alone. Oxygen tanks have requirements as well. They must be completely empty and flushed out with water before any cutting can begin. This emptying and flushing is best done by a professional. Contact your local compressed gas vendor for sources of spent tanks and hydro-flushing services.

Once you have a flushed tank, lay it on its side to measure and cut it. The best cutting tool for this job is a reciprocating saw. It is also possible to cut the tank with a small circular grinder fitted with a metal cutting blade, but it is harder to get a clean line going this route. If you do your layout wisely, you can get two containers out of each tank—one from the bottom portion and one from the cut-away top.

Once cut, the top edge must be ground clean of any burrs and other irregularities. This is the best time to employ the grinder. If you do not have a grinder, they are quite inexpensive to rent. Drainage holes must be drilled in or near the bottom of the cylinder. You can finish a steel tank container with paint and patina or paint by itself, or give it a ground, polished, sealed,

Several of the metal containers in the back garden were made out of expired oxygen tanks.

A steel pot made from an oxygen tank features a wax-resist style patina. *Photo by Connor Murphy-Levesque.* RIGHT *Asparagus densiflorus* (asparagus fern) tumbles down the front of a steel planter. *Photo by Connor Murphy-Levesque.*

shiny appearance. I chose to finish all of my steel pieces using the wax-resist method described in Chapter 3.

If the rigors of cutting compressed gas tanks seem a bit much for you but you desire the rough beauty of steel containers, you should be keeping an eye out for sections of large-diameter pipe or the more common material, scrap pieces of square steel tube. Square steel tubes come in a number of sizes, a good many of which are suitable for making planters. I constructed mine out of a short length of 6-inch-square tubing and finished it with a wax-resist finish. Mine was made to sit on a deck and required that a bottom be installed.

CAST-IT-YOURSELF CONTAINERS

Once you get the hang of projects like adding bottoms to tubes, the next thing to attempt is to cast your containers. A number of materials and methods are used to cast containers. The most popular do-it-yourself casting

INSTALL A BOTTOM ON A TUBE PLANTER

Installing a bottom on an open-ended tube regardless of shape need not be difficult, and to make sure that it is not I will share my secret recipe. You will need a roll of duct tape and a box of expansion cement (available at most hardware stores). If the diameter of your tube is 4 inches or greater, or your square tube is 4 by 4 inches across or more, you will also need a small amount of chicken wire or other malleable steel mesh.

1. Pick which end of your tube is to be the bottom and cover it completely with duct tape going from side to side, overlapping each piece of tape with the next. It is important that the tape be applied tightly and evenly with no gaps. It is advisable for larger volumes to tape a piece of cardboard that has been cut to fit the outside of your tube underneath the duct tape.

2. Insert into the top of the tube a thin wad of wire that is just slightly wider than the inside of the tube. Push down on it until it lodges just above the duct tape. It should not be pressed against the tape. If the length of the tube does not allow you to reach its bottom, or the inside dimensions prohibit getting the mesh into place easily, you can place the mesh in the bottom before taping. Take care that the mesh is completely inside the tube and will not contact the tape. This method may make it easier to install the wire mesh but requires a greater volume of cement.

3. Mix up the expansion cement as directed on the package. Expansion cement gets its name from the peculiar action it undergoes as it dries. Most cements shrink upon drying, but expansion cement is specifically formulated to expand, filling in completely the space where it is placed. This works just dandy for us.

4. Cover at least the majority of the wire mesh, if not all of it, with the cement. You will have to approximate the volume needed, but not to worry—this stuff is very forgiving. If you pour too little and your wires are still showing, simply mix and pour some more.

5. Stand the tube, bottom side down, on a hard flat surface and leave it there. Let the cement dry overnight. Then peel off the duct tape, and there is your brand new bottom. Be sure to drill at least one drain hole in the bottom.

Two hand-cast bowls hold a wealth of small succulents.

material is called hypertufa. So many recipes and sets of directions are available elsewhere that I am not going to further discuss this lightweight material. Instead I want to turn your attention to casting with exterior-grade plasters and cements. The easiest and most readily available of these durable plasters is sold under the "Fix-It-All" label. I am not usually one to endorse a specific brand, but this product has been very dependable over the years and works very well for casting.

A good mold material for casting planters is smooth plastic. Food storage containers, picnic ware, and plastic mixing bowls make excellent molds.

Secondhand ones from the thrift store are even better. The key to any good mold is flexibility; the material has to have a little give. If your mold is rigid, removing the finished container becomes more difficult, and you run the risk of breaking the mold getting the piece out. The other important factor is that the mold must be wider at the top, or at least no smaller than the body of the casting to be made. If the vessel you have in mind either has an inside lip at the top or tapers toward the top, this is not the item to use for a mold.

Having selected a suitable mold, you are ready to start the casting process. Casting containers in molds is a lot like making muffins. A number of the same rules apply. Your mold must be clean and free of dirt or other oils. Your work area should be clean. You should have all your ingredients and supplies ready and at hand before you start. The other similarity is that you have to "grease the pan." Cooking spray makes an excellent mold release. It is easy to apply, it stays where you spray it, and it does not cost much. A mold release such as the spray allows your new plaster container, or your muffins, to come out of the mold cleanly and easily.

Casting with exterior plasters allows you to incorporate decorative material into the body of the finished container. Because I manufacture tumbled glass products as part of my day job, tumbled glass seems to me an excellent ingredient, but it is by no means the only thing to mix in. Marbles, colored bits of plastic, stones, even old keys can be incorporated. The design decisions lie in your hands. If you want a lot of the additives to show on the outside of the finished container, you will need to first put a lot on the inside. This is because the plaster will coat and literally swallow a great portion of additives and you will never see them again.

The best way to estimate the approximate finished look is to premix your plaster and your additives first. Mix the dry plaster and additives in a large flat plastic pan, an old dishwashing tub, or a plaster mixing trough or similar vessel. It is important to remember how much plaster you are putting into the mix because you will need to keep the relationship of water to plaster the same as directed by the manufacturer on the package. This relationship holds firm even when you have incorporated your decorative additives. Adding extra water to accommodate the additives' volume only serves to weaken the plaster. The resultant mix must be fairly stiff, almost like slightly dry oatmeal.

Once your mold is sprayed with cooking spray and your plaster is mixed, it is time to pack it into the mold. Grab a good handful of plaster. Start at the bottom. Do not make the bottom of your container more than an inch

Casting with exterior plasters allows you to incorporate decorative material into the body of the finished container.

Inspired by a Chinese coin, this container is hand cast from exterior plaster.

thick to begin with. There is a reason for this—gravity. As you start to pack in plaster and build up the sides of your container, gravity will have its way. To defeat the effects of gravity you must do two things at the same time: pack in more plaster to build up the sides and pull up from the bottom to redistribute the plaster that keeps slumping toward the bottom. This sounds harder than it is.

As you pack the mold to the thickness of about an inch or less, the plaster will already begin to set and harden. It becomes a balancing act of packing wet material, spreading the slumping material back up, and getting it all done before the plaster hardens and becomes unworkable. I have found this to be a lot of fun, like making mud pies under a timeline. Get ready, get set, and go.

Once you have filled the mold, you have to leave well enough alone for a while. Two days is optimal. When the plaster has hardened and started its cure, you can gently coax the container out of the mold. This can be a telling moment. If you have done everything exactly right and in addition not offended any Greek gods this week, the piece will pop right out of the mold. On the other hand, if you were stingy with the mold release or are not that good at waiting for things to get done, you can have a less easy time extracting your new container from the mold. If it won't come out easily, you have to wait. There is no other way, short of cutting away the mold and risking—no, on second thought, not just risking but definitely scoring, scratching, and damaging the casting in the process. Wait a few days. As the casting sets up and dries it will shrink slightly, making the extraction that much easier.

Your cast container remains now only to be finished. You must decide what type and degree of finish you want for your new hand-cast beauty. Once cured, which takes about a week, the exterior-grade plaster can be shaped with a sander or grinder, or left as is. I have experimented with all three of these methods and found that the as-is option generally gives off an as-is look, more or less like you got that far with the project and then got bored. A sander will clean up edges, allowing you to roll the top lip into an organic curve or flatten it out to a crisp clean line. I generally seal my containers with exterior-grade water-based polyurethane. This slows down erosion from rain and garden hoses and helps seal the finished piece against dirt and staining. Be sure to drill one or more drainage holes.

This same process can be done using cement. Cement casting is done in the same way as plaster casting, with only a few variants. Cement dries at a different rate and is slower to cure. Cement casting requires the use of gloves and other safety gear, such as long sleeves, a dust mask or respirator, and eye protection. If you want the speed of plaster and the extra durability of cement, check out the plastic cements and cements that are advertised as rapid setting.

Cement and exterior-grade plasters both can be colored to suit a range of color schemes. Make sure the colorant you choose is compatible with the product you are using. If finished color is a major issue or you want some color that is not brown, black, gray, or green, plaster should be your product of choice. Plasters can take colorants ranging from commercial stucco colors to custom blends created with artists' acrylic paints. Color can be integrated directly into cements and plasters or applied as a coating once the casting is completed.

LARGE CONTAINERS, SMALL JOURNEYS

These are but a few of the ideas available to you when you design and build your own containers. The field is open, and the time is ripe to explore the options available to us as designers. What we build, repurpose, and cast is important. Each is a small journey; each can bring us closer to a new way of looking at our gardens and what they can become.

8

SITTING THIS ONE OUT

Building a garden is a great joy and a good deal of labor. Sometimes you need to stop, rest, and reconsider, which brings us to one aspect of garden and landscape design not to be overlooked, and that is seating. It seems a simple enough task to provide a good spot to sit for a moment or two out in your garden, but seating is often an afterthought. I have visited many gardens and have often found them lacking in sufficient, interesting seating. Most employ a store-bought bench plunked down unceremoniously in some corner or banished to the sidelines.

Unless your garden is very small, as in seriously tiny, it should offer more than one spot to sit down and enjoy it, more than one vista to embrace. Look at it this way: you spent all this time, and often no small sum of money, putting together your garden. What good is it if you cannot take full advantage of it, immerse yourself in its every aspect, and rest in it? It is of little good at all.

Reused materials offer a wealth of seating ideas. Materials can be repurposed, reimagined, and completely transformed into wonderful seating integrated into your landscape. Sometimes the opportunity for a good seating spot is right under your eyes, and the materials are already at hand just waiting for that bit of imagination, that little slip of the brain to bring it to fruition.

BACK PORCH BONANZA

One of the most popular spots to sit when we entertain in the garden was one of these very situations. Having refurbished the existing back porch by adding a new facing of steel skeletons and some curvaceous railing screens, I thought I was pretty much done, designwise, with that space. I had only to install a new top railing to cap the old one the skeletons were attached to, something I would get around to soon enough.

Then one hot afternoon my wife came out onto the porch to talk with me while I was installing some other aspect of the rear garden. She leaned on the railing for a few moments, then got up and went back inside to the kitchen. A moment later she returned with one of our Asian-style tall kitchen stools and a glass of cold white wine. After putting her wine on the railing, she pulled up the stool and sat down.

In one instant the porch railing had been transformed into a balcony bar. The only thing it needed was a wider top cap so we wouldn't need to balance our wine glasses on a 2x4. Having not yet found the exactly right material to use for a permanent 12-inch-deep countertop on the porch rail, I did the next best thing. I used what I had available locally—very locally. Two lengths of redwood 2x6 that had been part of the deck just below the porch were repositioned, cut to fit, and painted one of the accent colors.

The seats on the porch are always full when we have parties in the garden. Given the porch's proximity to the kitchen, it also makes a great spot for a midnight snack on hot summer nights.

BENCHES OUT OF BEAMS

The front garden has several seating areas built in. A half circle of vertical flat-topped stone forms an edge to the stone patio and provides seating. We installed an additional seating area on the outside edge of the garden, adjacent to the property line. This bench was constructed as both a visual extension and a terminus of the timber boxes that form the break between

An extra wide top rail on the back porch fashioned from used 2x6s and painted a bright accent color makes a good table for plates and drinks. *Photo by Connor Murphy-Levesque.*

the garden and the neighbor's lawn. The seat of the bench was built out of a large, heavy piece of laminate beam.

Laminated beams are used to hold up the ceilings in buildings where a large uninterrupted space is needed. The beams are common in basketball pavilions, gymnasiums, and similar open structures. Each beam is composed of layers of wooden boards joined together with adhesive under high pressure. These laminated beams are specifically engineered for each job, based on the load they must carry (the weight of the roof) and the overall span of the ceiling (how far the beam will carry that load between uprights or the outside walls). Laminated beams are made to be quite strong and very durable, even when exposed to the elements. These beams are shipped to the job site having not been trimmed to finished length. This allows the builder to make any last-minute adjustments to the length before installation. The factory ends are usually discarded, being far too short for most roofing jobs. They are not too short, however, to build benches out of.

The laminated piece used for the front garden bench was 12 inches thick by 21 inches wide by 40 inches long. I had rescued this chunk and now had a good spot for its use. I trimmed the beam flush and clean on both ends and installed it on a cribwork, or crossed stack, of 6x6 beams. The bench was set on a diagonal, facing across the entry path into the garden beyond.

Given its large size and substantial weight, the beam did not require much of an attachment to the cribwork below it, but to play it safe I secured it anyway. We in the San Francisco area have learned that it is best to anticipate a good shaking every now and then. This attachment was done by toenailing 3-inch screws from below—that is, placing the screws at a 45-degree angle to the 6x6 and then driving them upward through the edge of the 6x6 into the beam above.

Once secured, the bench was finished to match the timber boxes that abut it. A couple of wash coats of artist's raw sienna acrylic paint diluted in water formed the stain layer, which once dried was sealed with two coats of canola oil.

TOP This massive beam end will make a handsome and durable bench.
ABOVE The bench seat was installed on an angle to provide a better view of the front garden.

MAKE A LAMINATED-BEAM BENCH

To make a laminated-beam bench, you must first decide what type of beam to use. The laminated beam used to build the bench in my front garden is only one of several types of beams on the market. Historically, beams were composed of a single section of wood, cut from any number of types of trees. These beams are still around, and large specimens are prized not only for bench making but also for other architectural work such as mantle pieces and door arches. If you can find a section large enough to build a bench, a solid wood beam will make an enduring piece.

If you can't find a solid wood beam, the laminated beams are the next best choice, followed by composite beams. Composite beams or engineered beams are sold under a great many names. The basic version consists of large flakes of wood distributed throughout and laminated together under high pressure. These beams are engineered for weight to be brought to bear on the narrowest dimension, or edge, of the beam. When the beam is used for a bench seat, the weight is put on the broader face. Unless they are fairly short, composite beams can bow over time. This can be compensated for by distributing more support legs under the piece.

Next you need to decide how long a bench you want. Reclaimed beams are available in a great many lengths. Consider how much room you have to install the bench in, how you will transport the beam to your garden, and how the beam will be moved into place. A large beam can be very heavy. The piece used for the bench installed in my front garden is only 12 by 21 by 40 inches but weighs in at 250 pounds—well over 6 pounds a running inch! Really big beams may require a crane or construction forklift to maneuver them into place. Keep this in mind when shopping for bench beams. If lifts and cranes will not work for your budget there is always the Egyptian method, but let us not get ahead of ourselves by putting the cart before the beam.

Select a beam that is at least 12 inches front to back; this is a good minimum depth, as most of us are "broader in the beam" than this and prefer a deeper perch. Once you've selected your beam, proceed as follows.

1. If necessary, cut your beam to length, using rolling cuts as described in Chapter 7.

2. Decide what type of legs or bottom supports you are going to use and how long they need to be. A seat no lower than 14 inches off the ground and no higher than 20 inches will be comfortable for most people. A variety of materials can be used for legs. If you have sufficient length or more than one piece, you can carve the legs off of your chosen beam. You can also use cinderblocks, bricks, large flat pieces of fieldstone, inverted toilet tanks, old metal or wood milk crates, or short lengths of ceramic chimney flue. Supports can be set below grade to accommodate support heights.

3. Attach the legs to the seat. If you are using wooden supports, they can be attached via long screws or hex-headed lag bolts. The hardware can be hidden by (a) sinking the heads below the surface and filling the holes with wooden plugs cut from a small dowel, or (b) drilling countersink holes from the bottom of the leg and attaching it from below. If you are using concrete cinder blocks, milk crates, chimney flues, or other material that has a hollow center, these can be attached via long threaded bolts or rods that pass through holes drilled into the bottom of the seat beam and that are held in place at the base with large washers or metal plates and a nut at the end. If no easy method to attach the seat seems available, do not worry. The weight of the seat is often sufficient to keep it in place; gravity is the glue in this case.

5. Sand and finish the bench. For ideas on finishes, see Chapter 3.

6. Site and level the bench. Siting of your bench is important because where you put it will determine how and when it gets used. Consider how the view will change over the course of the day and year. Do not forget to consider what the night will reveal to you when you are seated there. Install your bench on level ground with good drainage, and make sure that the ground slopes away from your feet when you are seated.

7. Enjoy often.

Now, about the Egyptian method: any large heavy piece can easily be moved with three or four lengths of plastic or metal pipe 2 to 3 inches in diameter. The pipe should be no shorter than the widest part of what you are about to move. Begin by using a lever to insert three of the pipes beneath the beam in parallel, one each near the front, middle, and back, with the rounded edge facing the desired direction of travel. Leave a few inches to a few feet of beam overhanging the front and back pipes. Then using your lever, push on the beam from behind to roll it forward. Just before the back piece of pipe becomes exposed, insert the fourth length of pipe under the front of the beam. Push some more until the back pipe is no longer under the beam. Place this piece of pipe in turn under the front edge and push some more. Repeat until you arrive at your chosen site.

Because the bench was so close to the property line, I thought that some enclosure behind it would make it a more intimate spot. The bench forms the back edge of a paving area composed of a collage-like installation of round elements, so the circular motif was carried over into the surround materials. I chose to use a sheet of wood and a sheet of steel, both of which already had holes drilled out of them in pleasing patterns. The back panel is exterior-grade plywood sealed and painted to complement the house trim. It originally was part of the covering for a soundproof wall in an exhibit at a local science museum. The side surround sheet is a piece of 3/16-inch-thick steel that I had used in a few display gardens over the years. The steel is perforated with evenly spaced 1½-inch holes. It came to me by way of an acquaintance who does custom high-end metal fabrication. Generally involved in architectural commissions, he had made up this piece as a sample for a client who wanted the front of her residence covered in patterned steel. Her change of plans from circles to squares and his lack of storage room for stray materials was my gain.

The surround gives a seated person some sense of privacy while framing the garden view beyond. A good rest-and-read spot, the bench also makes an excellent place for talking with neighbors who drop by.

A small table placed by the laminated-beam bench picks up the motif of circular forms and perforations. The table base echoes the hose storage cylinder described in Chapter 4 while mimicking the garden bench surround's sea of holes. The table is composed of only two elements: a steel perforated pipe and a small piece of thick, round glass. The glass, which formerly had a glamorous life as part of a department store cosmetics display, balances firmly on the base and provides enough space for a cup and a book.

OPPOSITE Backed by panels, the bench offers a quiet spot to read.
ABOVE Made of only two components, this table is an easy and attractive project.

TIE IN A TABLE

Simple projects can be quite satisfying, particularly when the end result helps to tie different design elements in the garden together. Tying tables and benches together is particularly satisfying and by no means a difficult task. The trick is to create at least one point of commonality between the two pieces. This can be done by creating both in similar materials and scale, or by repeating a decorative or design element.

If, for example, your bench features a massive wooden seat, the table can echo that material and mass on a similar, or smaller but related, scale. If the setting precludes this, an alternative must be found. In my case I unified the mass of the bench and the slightness of the table through repetition of design elements. The bench's backing and the table's base both feature patterns of holes cut out of their surface. This relationship is further reinforced by the surrounding paving materials, which are all circular. In the case of the bench and table I placed under the arbor in my backyard, both have steel gabions as bases.

If neither related materials nor scale will work for you as unifiers, the one element left in your tool kit is color. Careful use of a single color scheme can bring unity to even fairly disparate pieces. Conversely, by accenting the differences that underlie a pairing, color allows texture and shape to take control of the picture. Either tactic can yield interesting effects worth exploring.

Made of a wood composite, this bench was a one-day project for my friend Sam Dorsey. A leg detail reveals the intricate patterns inside the compound material.

Compound materials such as laminated beams are becoming increasingly common in the construction trades, particularly as large structural-grade materials. This phenomenon is resulting in part from the dwindling supply of large timber to make beams from. Coupled with this are advances in the science of laminating materials to meet high-strength applications. A small bench designed and built by my friend Sam Dorsey employs a beam product composed of small flat chips of wood that are laminated together under

RIGHT Steel gabions wired together form a bench base. BELOW A larger gabion with a sheet of tempered glass on top becomes a cocktail table. *Photo by Connor Murphy-Levesque.*

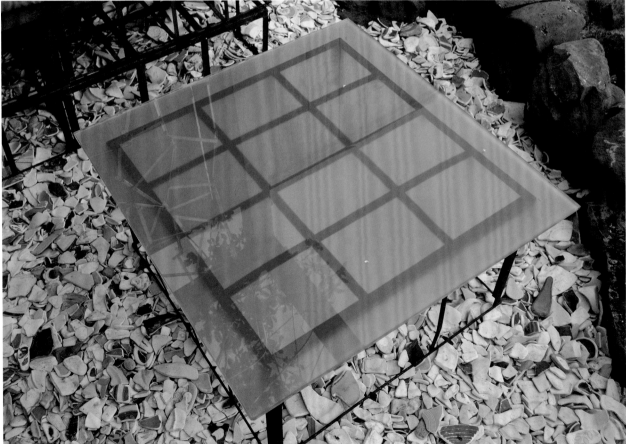

very high pressure. The resultant beam features complex and oddly beautiful patterns that this small bench shows off to good effect. Made in an afternoon, the bench was snapped up by an admiring passerby.

Outdoor cushions complete the seating area.

CONTAINER COUCHES

Sometimes it is the end product of multiple steps, such as the laminated wood products, that inspires us to create good garden seating. Sometimes it is the empty container left behind long after the contents have been put to use. The bench that graces the new arbor in my backyard is composed of four steel gabions. Recall from earlier chapters that gabions are like baskets or cages, originally used to hold up earthworks. The gabion form has been embraced for its strength in the construction of shipping containers for heavy materials. The gabions that make up the bench base here were used to transport decorative stone from China.

First I stacked two units, each measuring 8 inches high, side by side between the arbor uprights. I wired these base units together with a short piece of baling wire. Then I stacked two more gabions vertically above the others, wired them together, and wired them to the units below them. This provided a firm openwork base for some outdoor cushions. I topped an additional Chinese steel gabion, which had a taller profile, with a piece of secondhand tempered glass to make a low cocktail table. Both the bench and the table are simple in design but effective in use of materials at hand, and both are simply pleasing to look at and use.

STACKED SEATING

Sometimes a simple exploration of stacking methods can yield a design direction. Playing with just six short pieces of the same plastic-and-wood-composite material I used for my arbor yielded a fresh design for a seating area in the new front garden at Building REsources. The plastic-and-wood material, in the form of 4½-inch square tubes designed as post material for deck systems, lent itself to stacking.

Four pieces placed side by side made a pleasantly deep seating surface and were cut to length. Once the depth was established, short pieces running front to back were cut to fit, and two additional lengths were cut to form lower crosspieces. Stacking the cut material to make the finished piece took about ten minutes.

RIGHT A short stack of plastic-and-wood-composite tubes provided the inspiration for a bench. OPPOSITE The bench of stacked square tubes offers a resting spot in a newly constructed garden at Building REsources. Note the screen divider made of conduit; its construction was described in Chapter 5.

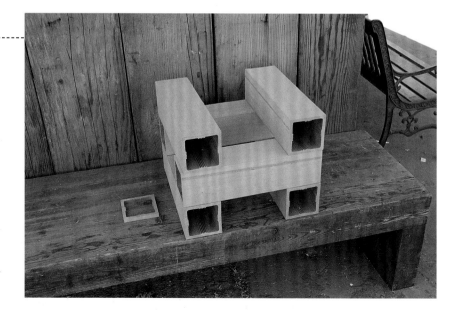

RIGHT Three PVC pipe sections installed at the edge of the back garden became a bench base. BELOW The pipe sections that serve as the bench base were backfilled with concrete scrap.

The unit was constructed on site and on grade. The only real work was to provide a level spot on which to set it. This challenge was met by reusing ¼-inch-thick perforated steel plate that had previously been cut into 1-foot squares. As described and illustrated in Chapter 4, this material was installed directly on leveled soil.

The units that make up this bench have yet to be glued together. The

Eyeglass lens blanks offer an unusual decorative solution to hide the scrap concrete in the lower portion of this bench support.

bench gets regular use and the dry stacked form has posed no problems to date. The entire process of conception, construction, and installation was completed in a single day with time to spare.

Stacking a seat of slats on top of cylindrical forms provided another easy seating solution in my back garden. I cut three sections of large-gauge, heavy-duty PVC pipe and installed them with their bases below grade. I leveled the portion left above grade at 16 inches, a comfortable sitting height. I backfilled the pipes with broken concrete scrap up to a height of about a foot. The bench top of open slats would permit a view down into the pipes from above. Consequently, I wanted to place some sort of decorative topping over the concrete to obscure it from view. What I ended up using were unground optical lenses, whose round forms complement the adjacent paving.

A fairly large volume of the lenses had been offered to me as scrap glass for tumbling into a decorative mulch but proved to be not well suited for this purpose. The glass had originated in Mexico, where it had been manufactured as eyeglass lens blanks. A glass artist in Oakland, California, had purchased them as surplus at a very steep discount and had them shipped to his studio. His intention, from what little I gathered, was to fuse the lenses onto sheets of flat glass, creating a low-relief bubblelike pattern. They apparently proved to be not well suited for this endeavor, either. They do, however, lend themselves to being an attractive surfacing material, which handily obscures the substrate when stacked several layers deep. The irony of using eyeglass lenses to obscure an unpleasant view was not lost on me.

The bench seat was donated to me free of charge by someone who dumped it illegally by the roadside. Made of black-painted wood slats spaced an inch apart, it was missing all of its legs, which had formerly been attached by means of four long, thin bolts protruding from the bottom. I removed these by cutting them flush to the wood with a reciprocating saw equipped with a metal-cutting blade.

The slats were held in place by three front-to-back pieces of wood, or stringer slats, that fell below the line of the seat. I marked where these fell when the seat was placed on the black pipe sections and cut notches in the tops of the pipes to allow the stringer slats to ride down so that the seat sits snug and level on top of the pipes. The bench makes a very pleasant

MATERIALS FOR STACKED SEATING

What kinds of locally available materials can be used for stacked seating? Let us begin to imagine.

- square steel or aluminum tubes
- heavyweight square-profile downspouts
- dimensional lumber, such as short lengths of 2x4s or 4x4s
- short sections of wooden beam
- wooden boxes
- shipping crates of various sizes
- old milk crates
- slabs of countertop stone (glued together as needed)
- wooden drawers from old cabinets
- suitcases (sealed with an exterior-grade water-based polyurethane)

Salvaged from a roadside dump, this bench seat was just the thing to stack on top of the sections of PVC pipe.

place to sit. It is another popular spot to gather when we entertain in the garden, especially at night, given its proximity to a dramatic lighting feature.

THINGS TO LOOK AT WHILE YOU SIT

Sometimes you just need a place to sit, and sometimes you need a place to sit and something interesting to look at while sitting there. Installations that use reclaimed materials to interact with rain, wind, and water make great focal points and are an area of the garden ripe for exploration.

In the case of our black bench, we placed immediately behind it a slender cylinder chosen to continue the circular motif. The acrylic tube measures 8 inches across and stands, above grade, just less than 5 feet high. A portion of the tube is set deep into the garden's soil and is both filled with and surrounded by crushed drain rock. The bottom half of the tube above grade is filled with lightweight black lava stone. Above this level, a portion of the tube is filled with more of the eyeglass lenses. This installation can seem, at first, purely a sculptural gesture. This perception gives way when the spiral rain chain mounted directly above the tube is taken into account. Then the truth of the issue becomes clear: it is simply a downspout, an elaborate way for water to descend from the roof and be conducted into the garden's soil. It is also a pleasurable way to enjoy the water's journey as it does. For all its other attributes, it is a downspout nonetheless.

Pulled out of the fire and left to the wind pretty much covers the use of gas water heater baffles in my garden. Water heater baffles are found only in gas-fired water heaters, where they are installed in the central flue. The baffle has one job to do in a water heater, and that is to slow down the escaping exhaust heat so that it can be transferred into the water before it goes streaming out the vent stack. It does this by forcing the rapidly expanding exhaust to go through a series of sharply curved turns.

Once extracted from the heater, the most common style of baffle reveals itself to be a single narrow ribbon of steel bent into alternating curves

Filled with eyeglass lens blanks, the acrylic downspout makes a dramatic statement. *Photo by Connor Murphy-Levesque.*

Planted like steel grass, these gas water heater baffles add visual as well as auditory interest to the garden.

every 3 inches or so. There is an alternate design, also fairly common, that employs a triangular bend instead of the curves, and one more that uses sharp 90-degree flanges to the same end. Which one slows down the heat best is best left up to the engineers. Which one is more attractive in the garden should be left up to your taste. I favor the curvy ones.

The color, rather the colors, that these baffles exhibit when removed from the flues is amazing. Reds, purples, oranges, and every shade of brown are on display. If left unsealed, the baffles generally and gently soften to a range of plum browns, which works fine in my garden.

LEFT Originally used to tie rowboats to, this aluminum sphere now anchors the arbor garden. *Photo by Connor Murphy-Levesque.* BELOW Rescued from a dumpster, this rusted sphere is a favorite piece of garden art.

My favorite use for these postindustrial gems is to plant them in the soil like so much steel grass. Planted in close proximity in a windy spot, they can provide a visual accent as well as perform a quiet clanging, clacking, and pinging music that I am getting fond of.

Wind also plays a part in making the cement pond in my rear garden as decorative as it is practical. The pond was originally installed free of charge in the late forties or early fifties by the county vector control. I live on a low, flat island in San Francisco Bay that historically had some drainage issues. Going hand in hand with the low, wet conditions was a large mosquito population, a circumstance that still can plague us to this day, though the drainage situation has gotten under control. To control the mosquitos, ponds were installed and stocked with free mosquito fish. This was not a bad solution to the problem and avoided the alternative, which I am given to believe was at the time spraying with a nasty and now illegal chemical. The pond is still there, and I am one of the few homeowners on my block who did not fill the thing in at some point with dime-store rosebushes. The mosquito fish are still free and still eat more than their share of larvae before the mosquitos mature and can take to wing. I am keeping the pond. But to add some visual interest, because the fish are very hard to see and slightly less than exciting, I have installed some floats.

Rearranged by the wind, three spheres are left to float in the pond beneath a welded steel hoop that forms a sculptural candleholder.
Photo by Connor Murphy-Levesque.

Two of the floats are lightweight copper spheres. Basically, these are oversized versions of toilet tank floats, which are fast becoming a thing of the past. Mounted in the toilet tank, the float would mechanically shut off the incoming water as it rose to a prescribed point. It did this by floating up on the incoming water. The float was attached to a lever that activated the shutoff valve. When the float came to the top of the tank it applied pressure on the valve, thereby closing it. When the toilet was flushed the float would drop to the bottom only to repeat its task. The floats I use never saw the inside of a toilet tank but they served the same function in larger systems such as storage tanks for boilers and radiator systems. The third member of the floating installation is a white, lightweight plastic sphere that was originally a round cover for a ceiling light. Freed of the ceiling, the light cover floats nicely. All three floats move at the will of the wind, forming and reforming arrangements of light and dark. This is made especially interesting at night.

The white plastic shade is of a large enough diameter to accommodate a single candle inside. I use aluminum-encased tea lights, which keep the flame low enough that the shade does not heat up measurably. I place the candle so its weight is at the bottom of the sphere, and the sphere's opening is at or near the top. This soft, low light dancing and weaving across even this small a pond enlivens the garden. The light bouncing off of the copper spheres adds a glimmer and furthers the effect.

A SEAT MUST BE SAT IN

All of these features in the garden—the benches, the tables, and the decorative elements—when built from reclaimed and reused local materials serve to illustrate only a small range of the design options available to us. They also serve to remind us that we have wasted good material, and valuable time as well, if we build what we will not use. A garden must be lived in. The furnishings must be used if we are to do anything at all with reuse through design. It is only through active use that we will learn what merely works, and what inspires us to go farther and farther in transforming our landscapes.

9

A CANDLE AGAINST THE NIGHT

There are many good books available on the subject of garden lighting and many beautiful lighting fixtures available for gardens and walkways and for almost every exterior lighting task imaginable. You can even get your faux waterfall backlit in an ever-changing rainbow of otherworldly hues. Yet when I ask avid gardeners and designers I'm addressing for a show of hands as to how many use their gardens at night, the response is completely underwhelming. In a group of twenty, there might be three hardy souls who venture out of the safety of the lair at night.

I find this utterly baffling. Here you have dedicated garden people who spend hours designing, building, and tending incredible gardens and then abandon them once the sun goes down. It is as if dragons might swoop down on them if they are caught out there without stadium lighting. I once had a women at a lecture tell me, with a completely straight face, that she did not go out into her garden at night because "there are animals out there." Imagine that, real animals moving through the real world in your lovely garden. Take a shotgun with you if you must, but get out there into the night.

YOUR GARDEN BY CANDLELIGHT

At night the garden takes on so many new and different shapes that daylight does not reveal. The tall back plantings in your borders are now the rustling edges of a fluid wall where leaf and darkness meet and dance. I recommend that if you do not currently use your garden at night, you begin that exploration tonight. It need not take long, and the benefits far outweigh the trouble of walking out your door. The one thing I will insist on is if you have one of those wall-mounted floodlights by the back door or on the garage wall, you turn it off and leave it off.

> At night the garden takes on so many new and different shapes that daylight does not reveal.

To explore your garden at night you need not have any lights on hand; in fact, the best way to explore your garden is by candlelight. Just like at dinner parties, everyone looks better in candlelight. If you do not have a candle lantern or hurricane lamp, do not despair; a tea light in an empty water glass works just as well. Make it a party. Bring several candles out and light up a path with them. Set them on the garden wall or next to your garden bench.

By moving through your garden at night with candles, you may discover that if it were turned just a little to the right, the bench would afford a great view of the moon through the dogwood tree. Or perhaps that if you put a small table and chair right there, you could sit and drink a cup of tea and watch the stars next to the rhododendron. I do not know what you will find; I only know that if you look you will find some spot in your garden that would benefit from being lit, and that if that spot were lit you would use it in some way at night.

SECONDHAND TECH LIGHTING

I use an inordinate number of candles in my garden. But I also use the latest in technology, as long as it is secondhand. For instance, I combined a garage sale set of solar-powered LEDs with a discarded cast resin shell. The tubular shell would have formed the outer covering for a sleek concrete contemporary planter but was badly cracked on the top lip. The parrot green material was a perfect foil for the LEDs, which tend to give off a cold blue-white light.

I buried the tubular cylinder upside down with the cracked portion below

ABOVE A set of solar-powered LED lights found at a garage sale provided the impetus for a combination table-lamp. LEFT The lights were placed at the bottom of a green cast-resin cylinder sunk into the earth. The wires exit through a tunnel under the cylinder edge.

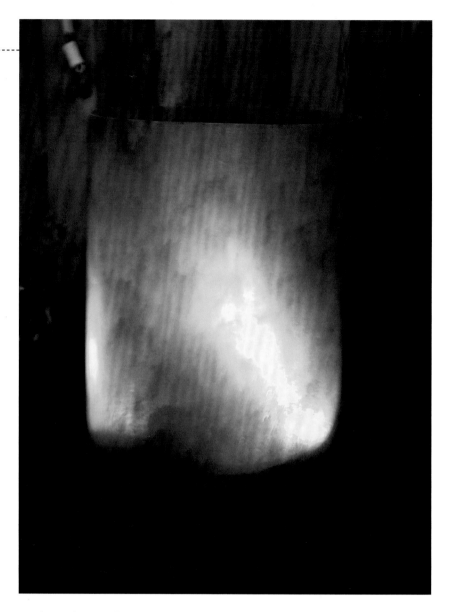

The LED lamps cast a solar-powered green glow at night.

grade to obscure the damage as well as provide firm footing for a glass table-top. I mounted the solar cells atop aluminum closet poles and fed the wires through a small tunnel under the back edge of the resin shell. I topped the installation with a 4-foot-round circular glass tabletop—another very local find, which I moved about 6 feet from its longtime home as my outdoor dining table (which I replaced with a salvaged glass top with an umbrella hole in it, something that the old top lacked). This combination side table

and lantern comes on just as the light fails and stays lit until almost sunup. I have gotten quite used to noticing its ethereal green glow when I get up in the night and glance out the window.

The only other electrically powered lighting in the rear garden is a plug-in version, turned on and off as needed. This vertical stack of three custom-made lamps held aloft by a simple wire gabion graces the small black garden between the house and the shed. I mentioned the construction of this lamp in Chapter 2 in my discussion of gabion-based designs. The gabion is a square tower about 3 feet high like a tomato cage and is built of black-painted hog wire. Hog wire is most commonly used in the construction of poured concrete driveways, where it acts as reinforcing mesh for the cement. It is a frequent visitor to reuse yards, because it is sold only in full rolls of 50 feet and most driveways do not require that much. The tower's wire grid plays off the grid of square glass-block paving that surrounds it, while the three lamps held by it play off the rounded forms in the rest of the garden.

Each of the three lamps consists of two hemispherical glass shades from old ceiling lights joined together with a black rubber and stainless steel band clamp, or hub as it is called in the plumbing trade, designed to seal

By day, the table-lamp (at right) provides another splash of green in the garden and another surface to perch an artistic candleholder on.

ABOVE, LEFT AND RIGHT A short length of rubber fuel line makes a weatherproof passageway through a plumbing hub for a strand of electrical wire.

the gap between two 12-inch water pipes. I found the glass portions first in a reuse yard. They feature a cast-faceted surface designed to give a sparkly effect like a cheap rhinestone. There was an apartment house hallway's worth of the glass shades available—actually more like a whole apartment building's worth.

I played around with them for a day or two and kept coming to the point where I would place them back to back, making a rough globe of them. I could easily glue them together in this position but I still needed to get the

RIGHT The plumbing hub is wired for a lightbulb. OPPOSITE Installed, the lamps sparkle and glow in their hog wire gabion.

necessary wiring and bulb in there. I also needed to be able to change the bulb every now and then, so that eliminated the idea of glue. The plumbing hubs provided the answer. The diameter of the glass shade fit perfectly into the hubs' open ends; the clamps could be tightened down to seal out moisture and loosened to facilitate changing the bulbs. The black-and-silver color scheme fit in with my design ideas for the garden. I also liked the contrast between the industrial toughness of the plumbing hub and the cheapness of the sparkly glass.

I fabricated the lamps on my dining room floor. I drilled a ⅜-inch hole in the center band of each of the three hubs and inserted a ¾-inch-long stub of automobile fuel line to thread electrical wire through. The fuel line acts a cushion so that the wires do not rub up against the sharp stainless steel of the band, and it also provides a weather seal. I fitted each fixture with a standard lightbulb base and a compact fluorescent lightbulb.

Some folks find the light from these fluorescent bulbs unattractive, but in this situation they perform perfectly. For my purposes I deliberately selected an undersized 13-watt bulb. This small-output bulb allows me to run all three lamps simultaneously without the garden looking like the inside of a warehouse store. The resultant light bounces off the lamps' facets and then off all the black and glass reflective surfaces in the garden, making for a dazzling but not overpowering display. The fluorescent bulbs do not build up nearly as much heat as standard incandescent bulbs would, which is a very important consideration in a sealed system like this. A standard bulb would burn out in days enclosed like this—or worse, start a toasty rubber-fueled fire.

CANDLELIGHT AND SHINY METAL

There is something primordial about firelight, and candles are just little fires. I love to use the soft, warm glow of candles bounced off of shiny metal surfaces. The metal surfaces of choice for me are stainless steel and bright aluminum.

Many of my stainless pieces come from surplus sales at universities. One of the local state universities has a large research hospital attached to it, and the surplus from this facility has some great shapes in it. Squares and rectangles abound, from small waste bin liners on up to some larger open-sided forms the original purpose of which I have yet to decipher. All of them will bounce candlelight around.

I like to put candles in the small square boxes and stack them one on top of another like a glowing minimalist sculpture. Some of the larger forms with multiple shelves, which I found out are used for holding equipment in

A pipette sterilizer does double duty as a candleholder.

an autoclave, look fantastic with a tea light on each shelf. Another piece of sterilizer equipment designed to hold pipettes doubles as a well-designed holder for 3-inch-diameter candles.

Another source for good shiny candleholders is used restaurant supply houses. I have bought some of my favorite pieces in these stores. These include an aluminum bucket full of holes that is not much good at holding

ABOVE A stack of small trash receptacles is filled with tea lights before dark. *Photo by Connor Murphy-Levesque.*
LEFT A collection of stainless steel vessels reflects candlelight into the garden.

This bucket-shaped colander from a used restaurant supply house is fitted with a large candle and mounted on a bracket to keep hot surfaces away from hands and shins.

CAUTION!
HOT SURFACES

Anytime you use a candle in a container not specifically meant as a candleholder, be aware of how heat might build up. Check out every one of your candleholder ideas in a controlled setting with gloves in hand. Due caution should always be exercised when using candles. They are quite lovely, but remember—they are only little fires.

in water and by the same token not much good at holding in light. The holes in its sides and bottom permit dime-sized streams of candlelight to escape, dappling any nearby surface with polka dots of light. I generally use this piece hung up—but not against a flammable surface, in part due to the heat it generates. The thing gets pretty darn hot, too hot to have down low where children or shins might touch it.

MORE CANDLE LAMPS

Sometimes the best candleholders are, well, candleholders. I bought some small glass votive holders at a hotel surplus sale. They had an odd feature: the bottom was not flat but had a glass stub that was molded onto the base and fitted with a small white ribbed rubber ring. A florist friend informed me that the holders were designed for banquets, where they could be used by sticking the stub into a traditional candlestick. Armed with that handy bit of knowledge, I set about finding something interesting to stick them into. I settled on chrome-plated steel closet poles. Three poles bought at a reuse yard were enough to make six pieces of varied length. It was simple to stick the holders into one end and then stab the other end into the soft soil near

the pond. Surrounded below by a swath of *Salvia darcyi* (Mexican sage), the candles form a small constellation that lends a soft glow in the middle of the garden. Sometimes you find these beautiful ready-made pieces and it is simply a matter of rethinking them, of putting them on a taller stand or in some cases turning them upside down.

The bases for the next candle lamps were a manufactured product. I do not know who built them, but I know they were built for the florist trade as stands for baskets and candleholders. The base is a small circle about a foot in diameter that supports a central shaft on three diagonal struts. The shaft is a single 5-foot-long steel bar that has been bent slightly here and there to give it a curvy profile. The top of the shaft is threaded, and here the original piece ends. I found two of these stands, and nothing that threaded onto them. I toyed with various objects bolted on top but found nothing that worked at all well. I put them in my shed for a while thinking something would come along that fit perfectly atop these curvy little things.

The solution arrived months later when I received a number of unfinished glass lampshades. Among the various shapes, some handblown and others machined, were a series of low conical forms intended for use as

Mounted at varied heights on closet poles, these hotel votive holders float above the garden.

On their chrome stems, candles light
a short walk to the house.

pendant lamps. One had a rough hole drilled in the bottom and others had no hole at all. I thought one might make a good salad bowl and dragged several of them home to concoct a base.

After breaking two of these glass pieces, I decided that they were too fragile for food service. So off to the garden with them for some as-yet unknown use. They did not stay in the garden, and my wife informed me she had put them in the shed with all that other stuff. There they were sitting on the floor, right next to the bases of the metal curvy stands. Sometimes it is just that way. The shapes aligned, the forms aligned, and the function aligned. In three minutes I had both of the stands driven topside down into the garden bed, and the conical glass resting perfectly on top of

ABOVE LEFT A glass lampshade and an upside-down metal stand make a candle lamp. *Photo by Connor Murphy-Levesque.* RIGHT This purple–black shade takes on a new look when lit with candles.

Large white spheres peek out through the plantings in the front garden.

them. I went in to get a couple of candles and found my wife at the door nodding her head in agreement. "Not bad" was all she had to say.

SPHERES OF LIGHT

The front garden is home to a group of seven large white spheres. Ranging in size from 12 to 20 inches across, the globe shapes are nestled into and among the plantings, causing some of the neighbors to describe them as my giant eggs. I like eggs; they have a pleasing organic form. If you hold up a candle to an egg, you can see what is inside and a soft glow comes out through them.

Each of these spheres lights up with a candle as well and gives off a very soft, warm glow. Considering these globes were used previously in shopping mall parking lots where their overbright, harsh light made them

Each sphere is lit with a single tea light.

unattractive at best, this is a welcome change. By limiting the candlepower to a single tea light, I avoid any overheating problems. The openings are more than large enough to exhaust a small candle's heat.

I have used spheres such as these in several gardens before, where I have run them on 12-volt, 7-watt yard lamps. This too is an effective way to underpower these large-diameter light globes. Simply point your 12-volt spotlight straight up and slide the lamp globe down over it. If you are using other styles of yard lights, these too can be housed inside large globes. Solar-powered lamps work well this way.

The spheres in my current garden are made of white plastic. Glass versions in various sizes are also available. I chose the plastic versions because there are small children in the neighborhood, and I do not wish to see their curious touches thwarted by a "that's breakable; don't touch" warning. Let them touch. Let them figure it out.

DO TOUCH

I am right there with the neighborhood children in many ways. But it is my own "don't touch" warning that I must avoid. It is my own "you cannot do that" voice that I must openly ignore and blithely brush past as I go about the business of reimagining what a garden can be. In order to truly rethink the garden, I have to get on with rethinking all the boundaries I set for myself—or worse yet, the ones I let be set for me. Boundaries imagined

Chondropetalum elephantinum (large cape rush) and *Phyllostachys aurea* (golden bamboo) share space in the garden with aloes, phormiums, and plastic light spheres.

or imposed keep us from improvising. They keep us from slipping past the known into the knowable.

We need a few less boundaries in the garden. We need more play, more dead serious play. We need to play with stuff and play really hard. We need to hunt down what is local, used, and readily available, and we need to drag it home and get busy playing with it. There are no lines we must play inside or outside of. In the end, in order to rethink the garden we must rethink the gardener.

GLOSSARY

ABS Acrylonitrile-butadiene-styrene, a class of plastics used to make pipe, computer cases, and other durable goods.

Asparagus densiflorus Asparagus fern, a feathery evergreen fern native to South Africa.

boiler core A heavy cast iron element used in series within a boiler to rapidly transfer heat to moving water.

bollard A heavy post used to impede movement past itself. Used in the construction of piers, or more commonly in front of government buildings to block vehicle traffic.

butt joint A woodworking joint composed of two pieces that abut each other at right angles. The material is cut square on the ends so that it meets the vertical surface of the opposing piece, to which it is fastened with nails or screws.

cemetery core A round piece of stone removed with a core drill from a headstone to allow installation of a metallic vase.

Chondropetalum elephantinum Large cape rush, a large grasslike plant from South Africa.

Crassula coccinea 'Campfire' Red crassula, a succulent native to the western cape of South Africa.

downstream shopping The practice of shopping for materials that are considered waste by the companies that generate or handle them and that would otherwise soon be in the waste stream, or the flow of materials away from the company's site and toward the landfill.

Dr. Seuss American author of children's books (Theodor Seuss Geisel, March 2, 1904 – September 24, 1991) who often drew fantastical buildings in his illustrations.

duckboard A platform of slats, often wooden, that allows water to drain away below the walking level, maintaining a dry walking surface.

Echeveria harmsii Plush plant, a succulent with velvet-plush leaves and red-orange to deep orange flowers.

Festuca glauca 'Elijah Blue' Blue fescue, a blue-green grass that forms spiky clumps.

flashing A thin metal sheet, often aluminum, sold in roll form and used to weatherproof seams under roofing materials, particularly where two angles or planes abut.

hardscape Those constituent parts of a garden or landscape that are not plant material, such as paths, trellises, and other structures.

hub A plumbing connector designed to join two sections of pipe together and prevent leakage, often composed of malleable materials such as rubber and steel banding.

kusari doi Rain chain, a Japanese alternative to the Western-style downspout that allows the descending water to be seen and heard as it travels down and through the links.

LED Light-emitting diode, an electronically controlled light source that generates almost no measurable heat, has a very long bulb life, and uses very little energy.

Leucadendron salignum Conebush, an evergreen shrub from South Africa with red-tinged leaves and stems.

minideck A wooden decklike structure often used in series that falls somewhere between the scale of a stepping-stone and a full deck, ranging from 4 to 30 square feet in size.

Miscanthus sinensis 'Gracillimus' Eulalia or maiden grass, a large showy grass that grows to 6 feet or more in height and 4 feet in girth.

miter joint A woodworking joint where two members, each with an end cut at a 45-degree angle, are joined to form a 90-degree joint.

monument maker A craftsperson who produces cemetery headstones and markers.

Nevelson, Louise Russian-born American sculptor (September 23, 1899–April 17, 1988). Born Leah Berliawsky, Ms. Nevelson created a large body of work in an expressionist vein from bits and pieces of wood that she found on the streets. Often finished in a monochrome, most famously black, her work goes well beyond simple collage and is collected by institutions throughout the world.

patina A coating such as rust or other oxide on the surface of a metal.

Phormium tenax 'Atropurpureum' Purple-red flax, a member of the flax family noted for its bronze coloration.

Phyllostachys aurea Golden bamboo, a densely leafed, thin cane bamboo well suited to pots; it will reach up to 15 feet in the ground, slightly less potted.

pick-up sticks A child's game, also known as jackstraws, involving a series of thin sticks that are dumped into a pile from which they must be extracted. Some sets feature a small steel band at the center of each stick and the extraction is done via a small magnet.

pipette A narrow plastic or glass calibrated tube used to draw up fluids in medical and scientific settings.

Pseudosasa japonica Japanese arrow bamboo, a tightly grouped, narrow stalk bamboo, reaching 15 feet, with large green leaves.

PVC Polyvinylchloride, a group of plastics used in piping, wire insulation, and a host of other applications.

repurposed Descriptor for an object or material used for something other than its intended purpose.

reuse The act of using a material in its original form but not necessarily for its original purpose.

reuse facility A store or materials yard that specializes in the sale of salvaged, reused, and secondhand materials. Almost any category of materials can be found in this type of setting, but the term is often associated with building material salvage stores.

rustification Building or finishing a new item in a manner that deliberately makes it appear to be rustic or "shabby chic." This includes but is not limited to strategies such as cracking and distressing finishes or sanding through paint to create the look of age and wear.

Salvia darcyi Mexican sage, a clumping sage that features long soft gray-green stems studded with small purple florets that attract hummingbirds.

Senecio vitalis Blue chalk fingers, a succulent that is a fast and easy grower in warm to moderate climates.

skeleton The remaining piece of stock, either steel or plastic, left over after parts have been cut out of a flat sheet by means of either a laser or a water jet.

slag glass The cooled cast-off glass left over from casting operations, characterized by rough, sharp edges and irregular forms caused by its rapid, almost explosive cooling.

slippage Based on the concept that the brain uses analogies to construct our ability to know what something is, either physically or in the realm of ideas, slippage argues that the brain can either accidentally or purposely slip past the known image and land somewhere else, thereby forming a new analogy—a new "this is like that" image.

surplus sales Any of a number of institutional or commercial sales where excess or outdated supplies or equipment is sold off at a discounted price.

tumbled glass and ceramics Broken glass and/or ceramic material that has been tumbled in a drum to remove any sharp edges. The material is turned either with water or with water and a number of aggregates such as sand. The resultant product has a soft finish, reminiscent of glass that washes up on beaches, and can be used as mulch, decorative topping material, or walkway gravel.

Uniola paniculata Sea oat, a clumping grass very tolerant of salt air, with drooping stems that end in clusters of chevron-shaped seed heads.

waste stream The entire flow of waste materials from residential, business, and industrial sources toward the landfill.

wax resist A method of making patterns on a surface by using wax to block out the colorant or coloring agent and then melting the wax away.

Wright, Frank Lloyd American architect, author, and lecturer (June 8, 1867–April 9, 1959). An early proponent of organic architecture, unitized housing, and anchoring a building in its landscape.

Zantedeschia sprengeri A calla lily with a deep purple-red bloom.

RESOURCE GUIDE

Given the inseparable relationship between what you build and what you build it of, when working with local reuse it is important to know where to look for materials. The real answer to this question is that you look everywhere, that you keep your eyes and imagination open whenever you are out and about. Use your newfound downstream shopping skills to discover who has what you need right in your own neck of the woods. Here is a short list of places to start. Happy hunting!

NATIONAL ORGANIZATIONS, UNITED STATES

Building Materials Reuse Association

This is a great resource for finding out who in your area sells reused building materials. The Web site lists not only the members of the Building Materials Reuse Association, but also almost every outlet the United States in its state-by-state listing. It even adds in a few Canadian listings for good measure.
www.bmra.org

Freecycle

The Freecycle Network is a nonprofit grassroots movement of people who are giving and getting stuff for free in their own towns. "It's all about reuse and keeping good stuff out of landfills." Check the Web site to find a group near you.
www.freecycle.org

Habitat ReStore

This is far and away the largest single chain of reuse stores throughout the United States and Canada. An outgrowth of Habitat for Humanity, a nonprofit that builds low-cost housing, the ReStores carry a wide variety of useful materials. Check the Web site to find the ReStore closest to you.
www.habitat.org/restores.aspx

SalvoWeb

SalvoWeb includes an online directory "for people in search of antique, reclaimed, salvaged and green materials for gardens and homes."
www.salvo.us

REGIONAL CENTERS, UNITED STATES

Stardust Building Supplies
4240 W. Camelback Road
Phoenix, AZ 85019
(408) 668-0566
www.stardustbuilding.org

Building REsources
701 Amador Street
San Francisco, CA 94124
(415) 285-7814
www.buildingresources.org

The Resource Yard
2665 63rd Street
Boulder, CO 80301
(303) 419-5418
www.resourceyard.org

The Green Project
2831 Marais Street
New Orleans, LA 70117
(504) 945-0240
www.thegreenproject.org

The Loading Dock
2 North Kresson Street
Baltimore, MD 21224
(410) 558-3625
www.loadingdock.org

The Reuse Center
2801 21st Avenue South
Minneapolis, MN 55407
www.thereusecenter.com

Build It Green NYC
3-17 26th Avenue
Astoria, NY 11102
(718) 777-0132
www.bignyc.org

Building Value
4040 Spring Grove Avenue
Cincinnati, OH 45223
(513) 475-6783
www.buildingvalue-cincy.org

The Rebuilding Center
3625 N. Mississippi Avene
Portland, OR 97227
(503) 331-1877
www.rebuildingcenter.org

Renew Building Materials
and Salvage Inc.
16 Town Crier Drive #2
Battleboro, VT 05301
(802) 246-2400
www.renewsalvage.org

Second Use Building Center
7953 2nd Avenue South
Seattle, WA 98108
(206) 763-6929
www.seconduse.com

REGIONAL CENTERS, CANADA

Jack's New and Used Building Materials
4912 Still Creek Avenue
Burnaby, BC V5C 4E4
(604) 299-2967
www.jacksused.com

National Building Supplies
22903 Sutton West
Ontario, MB L0E 1R0
(905) 473-3462
www.nabusu.com

Renovators Resource
6040 Almon Street
Halifax, NS B3K 1T8
(902) 429-3889
www.renovators-resource.com

Eco Reno
6631 Papineau Avenue
Montreal, QC H2G 2X3
(514) 725-9990
www.ecoreno.com

NATIONAL ORGANIZATIONS, UNITED KINGDOM

Recycle for Wales
Created as part of the Waste Awareness Wales campaign, this Web site allows users to search for where building materials can be recycled or picked up for reuse in Wales. The Web site is bilingual (English and Welsh) and very easy to navigate.
banklocator.wasteawareness-wales.org.uk

ReIY (Reuse It Yourself)
This site represents a UK-wide network of material reuse centers that collect and resell excess construction materials. There is also a sister Web site, BioRegional Reclaimed.
www.reiy.net/
www.bioregional-reclaimed.com/

Reuze
A great introduction to recycling in the UK can be had on this Web site. There are pages where you can advertise items you want to find or pass along, and many links to other

organizations involved in both recycling and reusing a wide range of products.
www.reuze.co.uk

SalvoWeb UK

This site is a gateway to the world of salvaging antiques and other architectural materials. The homepage provides links to many organizations in the UK that specialize in reclaimed building materials.
www.salvo.co.uk

UK Freecycle

This site for UK Freecycle groups matches people who have things they want to get rid of with people who can use them. The group aims to reuse and recycle existing products so as to reduce consumerism and encourage the manufacturing of fewer goods.
www.uk.freecycle.org/

LENGTH CONVERSIONS

inches	centimeters		feet	meters
1/8	0.3		1/4	0.08
1/6	0.4		1/3	0.1
1/5	0.5		1/2	0.15
1/4	0.6		1	0.3
1/3	0.8		1 1/2	0.5
3/8	0.9		2	0.6
2/5	1.0		2 1/2	0.8
1/2	1.25		3	0.9
3/5	1.5		4	1.2
5/8	1.6		5	1.5
2/3	1.7		6	1.8
3/4	1.9		7	2.1
7/8	2.2		8	2.4
1	2.5		9	2.7
1 1/4	3.1		10	3.0
1 1/3	3.3		12	3.6
1 1/2	3.8		15	4.5
1 3/4	4.4		18	5.4
2	5.0		20	6.0
3	7.5		25	7.5
4	10		30	9.0
5	12.5		35	10.5
6	15		40	12
7	18		45	13.5
8	20		50	15
9	23		60	18
10	25		70	21
12	30		75	22.5
15	38		80	24
18	45		90	27
20	50		100	30
24	60		125	37.5
30	75		150	45
32	80		175	52.5
36	90		200	60

INDEX

ABOUT THE AUTHOR

CREDIT: PHILIP B. MITCHELL

A pioneer in the art of using recycled materials in cutting-edge garden design, Matthew Levesque is the program director and master of recycled art at the non-profit San Francisco company Building REsources. An award-winning presenter at the San Francisco Flower and Garden Show, he teaches many popular workshops on creative reuse in the garden and landscape. His custom artwork, furniture, and lighting is sought by garden designers, as is the stunning tumbled recycled glass available through Building REsources. An accomplished builder and remodeler as well, he has appeared on HGTV, the Discovery Channel, the San Francisco CBS affiliate, and other local broadcasts. Matthew lives in Alameda, California.